The
Man Fast

Love Yourself Through God's Eyes, Heal Brokenness,
Break Soul Ties, & Prepare For The Man Of Your Prayers.

DR. TAMIKA HALL

Published By: TamikaINK

Library of Congress Cataloging-in-Publication Data has been applied for
ISBN: 979-8-8691-1197-5
PRINTED IN THE UNITED STATES OF AMERICA

Table of Contents

PART IV

Becoming The Good Thing

PART I

Reclaiming My Heart

Introduction

At the time of writing this book, it's been seven months since God put me on a Man Fast. I was in the nail salon, my feet soaking in the pedicure basin, foil around my fingernails, and I'd just turned on a movie to relax.

"Give me one year. No distractions..."

Using my knuckle, I turned off the movie that hadn't even gotten past the opening credits and took my AirPods out of my ears. Leaning my head back on the massage chair, I asked, "What did you say? Papa, was that you, or am I just being deep?" Surely, I'd heard God wrong.

Let's be clear, I wasn't dating. I hadn't even been on a date in almost two years; there was someone who was attempting to reenter my life, and I thought that his reentry was an answer to prayer – so when He spoke to me, I was confused – willing to obey but still confused.

Papa repeated Himself, *"Give me one year, no distractions."*

It wasn't a mistake. I'd heard Papa correctly. So, without hesitation, I responded, "Yes, Sir."

When I gave Him my "yes," He continued, *"Give me one year, no distractions. Watch me blow your mind. One year. Love, wealth, real estate. You will lack nothing. Make room for me, and you will never be empty."*

Saying "yes" was easy for me, but days later, the reality of waiting another year had me dissolve into sobs, "Haven't I been waiting long enough? Lord, did I do something wrong? Haven't I been serving you well already?"

Papa lovingly responded, "I'm going to teach you to seek validation only from me. He will love and adore you. Let me complete the work. You don't see how I will do it, but I will do it. I am the wraparound God."

I had to research "Wraparound God" and found it in Psalms 18:30 TPT (The Passion Translation), which says, *"Yahweh, what a perfect God you are! All Yahweh's promises have proven true. What a secure shelter for all those who turn to hide themselves in you, the wraparound God."* In this verse, the word "wraparound" is translated to be a shield of protection.

Wow, what a perfect, wonderful, loving God we serve that He allowed me to be His daughter and share my frustration. Instead of being angry, He explained that my heart and the things I desire matter so much to Him that He wanted to literally wrap around or protect me so that He could complete the work not only in me but in my future spouse as well.

I declare that God is wrapping himself around your life. He is healing your heart, mind, and emotions and fulfilling your desires. I declare that you will know what freedom feels like and that you will walk in wholeness. And as God completes the work in you, He is doing the same in your future life partner. Let Him be your shield.

Let me tell you a secret: fasting doesn't do anything for God; it's what *you do* to draw closer to Him. Fasting helps you discipline your body so that it doesn't control you, but you can bring it under subjection. True fasting (one meant for connecting with God) is not to be treated as a diet to lose physical weight but one that helps you lay aside every weight and distraction that keeps you from building a relationship with God (Hebrews 12:1).

You may be embarking on a Man Fast because God told you to, or you want to draw closer to God. Perhaps it's because, after years of abuse, your heart can't take another blow. Maybe it's because you're tired of choosing the wrong men. I can promise you that if you commit to the process and let God heal you, you will see a shift in your life.

Let me warn you: the moment you make this commitment, it isn't always going to be easy. Men may come from every area code; your flesh will get hot (you will want sex), you may get irritated and feel lonely, etc. Know that these are fleeting. I want to encourage you not to get caught up in these happenings because they are merely distractions.

YOU ARE WORTH THE PRESS. If you push through, you will begin to see yourself the way God sees you, and your self-esteem will shoot through the roof! You will love yourself differently, you will establish healthy boundaries, and your appetite for what you desire in a relationship will change.

There will be moments that you won't like the fast for different reasons. It may be because you love having a man around. Or maybe the uneasiness will come from being honest with yourself *about* yourself. But the payoff will be sweet – if you do the work, you'll be so proud of yourself. If a relationship follows, the person you connect with is going to have a better version of you.

I love you and want you to win. This book is like your own literary counseling session with me as your personal cheerleader and coach. I have included a few sections within each chapter:

- **Reflection Activities & Questions**: most chapters contain activities and/or questions (or both). Some activities will be easy for you to complete, others may take you a few days, and that's ok. You will be facing yourself in the mirror, confronting some hard truths, and ultimately offering them to God for Him to refine you.

- **Prayers of Deliverance and Strength:** Each chapter ends with a prayer that is scripturally accurate and aids in the deliverance process of the fast. Each scripture builds onto the previous one, so don't skip ahead and make sure to complete all work within the chapter to get the most out of each word spoken.

- **Scripture Roundup:** During this fasting time, it is important to spend time in the Word daily. Each chapter ends with scripture from within the chapter to aid in your daily devotion. This builds your relationship with God, strengthens your resolve to complete this fast, and it fortifies your spiritual armor against the enemy. Chapters where there aren't many scriptures used, additional scripture will be given.

  Hebrews 4:12 says, *For the word of God is quick, and powerful, and sharper than any twoedged sword, piercing even to the dividing asunder of soul and spirit, and of the joints and marrow, and is a discerner of the thoughts and intents of the heart.* In other words, the Word of God is so powerful that it will expose our innermost thoughts and desires, and change will begin to happen before we even realize it. So, pull out your Bible and pen, and watch how your spiritual life takes off.

The Reflection Activities, Prayer, and Scripture Round Up have been crafted to make you examine yourself and pull out toxic actions, beliefs, thought patterns, etc., to present them to God for Him to provide healing and deliverance.

Chapter One
What Does A
Man Fast Look Like?

When God first told me to give Him a year, a person I loved had come back around after about a year and a half of our not seeing each other. I was confused because I thought God had sent him back to me and that he was ready for a commitment. When he returned, I was clear that things weren't going to be the way that they had been when we were entertaining each other before. The main thing was that I was NOT having sex. At first, I was able to maintain that stance, but our conversations turned raunchy; we were having phone sex, and I wasn't sure how much longer I would be able to hold out.

So, when God put me on a Man Fast, I asked Him, "What does that look like? I don't want to be disobedient. Does that mean I have to stop talking to him and seeing him?"

Papa didn't respond. I can laugh at it now because the answer should have been obvious, but I wanted what I wanted. And I *wanted* God to tell me that I could still have conversations and meet-ups *while* fasting from men. I know, you probably rolled your eyes, didn't you? Yes, it was silly, but it's true.

If you are being called to a Man Fast, understand that God loves you SO MUCH that He wants to spend time with you so that you can get to know Him as your *father*. A father who wants the best for you and wants to show you how He sees you so that you can hold yourself in higher regard. A Man Fast will completely reset your thinking about love – starting with what it means to truly love yourself.

Fasting will look different for every person, but I believe there are some basic "rules" to it:

1. **Fasting From Food.** We see where people fast from all sorts of things – social media, shopping, television, etc. That's fine, but a true Biblical fast is one that includes fasting from food. In the Bible, you will see every fast marked by the abstinence of food. It is a sacrifice that God honors. I believe that unless you are participating in a corporate fast, fasting is between you and God.

   I fasted for the first five months of my Man Fast every day from 6 AM to a designated stopping time. Initially, I didn't have a time frame for my fast; for example, I didn't say, "I'm going to fast for seven days," I put the stopping point in the Lord's hands, and it ended up being five months. I had spent much of my life surrendering to my flesh, and I knew I needed to beat it into subjection (1 Corinthians 9:27)

When the Lord told me to stop, I did. After that, I would put myself on a fast *the moment* I felt that my flesh was rising up. Not just having outright sex with someone, but anytime I felt like I was going to give into masturbation, watching porn, etc.

2. **Intentional Connection With God.** If you aren't going to build with God, then what is the point? This will be just like the person who goes on a fast and tells everyone for attention when their real intention is to lose ten pounds. I immediately jumped into building a relationship with God through daily devotion, prayer, and fasting. It made the process more bearable. There will be days that you want to end this process, but your relationship with God will anchor you. There is nothing more beautiful than the love you are about to discover.

3. **Abstain From Romantic Relationships.** The point is to give yourself time to heal and recalibrate from relationships. Understand that Satan will pull out all of the stops to derail your fast, and you may find a host of men trying to date you. Don't be confused and think this is God's doing. If you set a time frame for your fast, honor it, and know that God isn't going to break the covenant that you've established with Him. God isn't going to tempt you to break your fast; He doesn't do that. I'm not saying that you won't

encounter your forever partner during this time because I can't speak for the mysterious ways of God, but that isn't your focus, and guess what? If God sent Him to FIND YOU, He will be waiting when your fast is over.

4. **ZERO Dating Activity.** This is not the time for phone conversations, text messages, DMs, etc. You won't be going on any breakfast, lunch, or dinner dates in an attempt to get to know the other person. During my fast, I didn't speak to men on the phone. I'm not talking about true friends, I'm referencing those who had an attraction to me, or there was a mutual attraction.

5. **Self-Discovery.** When the mirror was held up to my face throughout my fast, I had to be honest about what I saw reflected there. It didn't matter that I was preaching around the world, prophesying, and empowering women; I had a level of insecurity that led me to engage in attention-seeking behavior. Prepare to look in the mirror.

6. **Redefine Thoughts and Actions That Take You Away From God.** As you grow, your daily thoughts and actions will change as well.

7. **Spiritual Growth**. You are about to SOAR! Get ready for miracles, signs, and wonders to begin

manifesting in your life. There are blessings attached to righteous living. Proverbs 10:6a tells us that *blessings are on the head of the righteous...*

WHAT DOES FASTING DO?

Isaiah 58:6b says, *"...to loose the bands of wickedness, to undo the heavy burdens, and to let the oppressed go free, and that ye break every yoke?"* In other words, fasting accomplishes four things:

1. **Break the bondage of wickedness (evil, iniquity, guilt)-** Sin opens the door for the enemy to wreak havoc in our lives, and it restricts forward movement in all areas of our lives. Fasting breaks those chains.

2. **To undo heavy burdens.** A burden is oppressive and causes worry, guilt, shame, etc. Fasting lifts the weight of the burden.

3. **Let the oppressed go free.** Another word for "undo" is "free." If fasting lifts the weight of the burden, it frees the one fasting from the oppression associated with the burden.

4. **Breaks every yoke.** An actual yoke is a piece of wood put around a bull so that it can be controlled and moved wherever the yoke is pulled. Ever found yourself falling into sin even though you didn't want to? Fasting has an

amazing result: it breaks yokes that control and hinders our lives.

<u>BENEFITS OF FASTING</u>

There are many benefits of fasting listed in Isaiah 58:8-16:

> *⁸ Then shall thy light break forth as the morning, and thine health shall spring forth speedily: and thy righteousness shall go before thee; the glory of the Lord shall be thy rereward.*
> *⁹ Then shalt thou call, and the Lord shall answer; thou shalt cry, and he shall say, Here I am. If thou take away from the midst of thee the yoke, the putting forth of the finger, and speaking vanity;*
> *¹⁰ And if thou draw out thy soul to the hungry, and satisfy the afflicted soul; then shall thy light rise in obscurity, and thy darkness be as the noon day:*
> *¹¹ And the Lord shall guide thee continually, and satisfy thy soul in drought, and make fat thy bones: and thou shalt be like a watered garden, and like a spring of water, whose waters fail not.*
> *¹² And they that shall be of thee shall build the old waste places: thou shalt raise up the foundations of many generations; and thou shalt be called, The repairer of the breach, The restorer of paths to dwell in.*

Let's break down this list of benefits:

1. Physical and spiritual restoration and rejuvenation will happen quickly, and God will

be like a wall of fire around you to protect you (Isaiah 58:8).

2. When you cry out to the Lord, He will respond (Isaiah 58:9).

3. If you bless (give to) the poor/less fortunate during your fast, God will cause you to shine in dark places (Isaiah 58:10).

4. God will guide you and help you press through tough times. He will refresh and strengthen you when you feel depleted. (Isaiah 58:11).

5. You will break Generational curses, reset your bloodline, and God will call you "The Repairer Of The Breach," "The Restorer Of Paths to Dwell In." (Isaiah 58:12)

There is much to fasting, and while turning down your plate and abstaining from things your flesh wants to do can be a challenge, the benefits far outweigh the sacrifice.

You are not obligated to tell people you are on a Man Fast; that is your personal business. If someone asks you on a date, you can simply say, "Thank you, but I'm not dating right now." You don't owe anyone an explanation beyond that.

Establish Your Man Fast

So, what will your Man Fast look like? You will want to make the decision, set a time frame, establish goals for your fast, determine what you would desire to see when the fast has been completed, and dedicate the fast to God.

1. **How long will your Man Fast be?** This can be months or year(s) _______________________

2. **What are the terms of your food fast?** (For example, you might say, *"I will fast the duration of my Man Fast every day from 6 AM-Noon, with no food or drink during my fast time. Water only if I need it. After my fasting time, I am able to eat whatever I want."*)

____

____

____

____

____

____

3. **Why are you embarking on a Man Fast?**

____

____

____

____

____

4. Define your wellness goals <u>during</u> the fast:

You will be amazed at how quickly you are able to gain clarity, refresh, restore, and excel when you remove *yourself* from distractions. I want you to carefully consider what you would like to accomplish in your life spiritually, emotionally, intellectually, creatively, physically, occupationally, financially, socially, and environmentally.

Feel free to take your time to complete this section, but *it is* important. So often, we "fly by the seat of our pants" through life without considering our thoughts, needs, and desires, and it can leave us feeling helpless. I remember taking time to reflect on these areas of my life, and I became so excited to see how I would feel on the other side of *the process*.

What are your **spiritual** goals?
(How will you deepen your relationship with God?)

____

____

____

What are your **emotional** goals?
(Do you effectively cope with life? How do you connect/create satisfying relationships? Is therapy something you need?)

____

____

____

What are your **intellectual** goals?
(Do you desire to expand your knowledge or skill in a particular area?)

____

____

____

What are your **creative** goals?
(Is there a talent or creative side of yourself that you've neglected or never explored?)

____

____

____

What are your **physical** goals?
(How are your sleep habits, exercise habits, and overall health? Do you need to do a better job of taking care of YOU?

____

____

____

What are your **occupational** goals?
(Do you desire to grow or change jobs? Want to launch or expand a business?)

____

____

____

What are your **financial** goals?
(How is your credit? Do you want/need to pay down debt? Do you have a savings goal?)

____

____

____

What are your **social** goals?
(Do you feel like you belong, or do you need to work on connecting? Do you have a support system?)

____

____

____

When the fast is over, what do you want to have accomplished? _______________________________

____

____

____

____

____

____

____

____

____

____

____

____

____

Man Fast Declaration

Father, cover me as I embark on this journey of self-discovery. Give me peace when things get hard. Be my comfort when I feel lonely. I invite you into every broken place of my heart. Please mend my heart. Give me hope, restore my joy, and fill every empty space.

Lord, I dedicate this fast to you.

I present the next ________________Months/Year(s)   to you with no distractions.

This fast is necessary at this moment in my life because

____

____

____

____

My overall goals for this fast are

____

____

____

____

When I complete this fast, I want to be proud of myself for _____________________________________

____

____

____

____

Complete the prayer in your own words...

There are gems in the word of God. Take time to study your word daily. Here is a list of scripture from within the chapter to get you started.

- Psalms 18:30 TPT
- Hebrews 12:1
- Hebrews 4:12
- 1 Corinthians 9:27
- Isaiah 58:6-12
- Matthew 17:21
- 2 Samuel 3:35

Lord, as I reflect on your word for my life, my thoughts are: ________________________________

____

____

____

____

____

____

____

____

____

____

The scripture(s) that resonated with me the most:

____
____
____
____
____
____
____
____
____
____

I will apply the scripture to my life by:

____
____
____
____
____
____
____
____
____
____

Chapter Two
The Fastest Way to Get Over A Man is to Get Under the _Right_ One

"*ursue ME and let him pursue you,*" That was the answer God gave me after the heartbreak that catapulted me into purpose. I had been dating someone for almost a year. Wait, let me change that, I had been dating someone who *wasn't* dating me for almost a year. Have you ever found yourself in that situation? When you thought you were in a relationship only to find out the other person never saw it that way? Yep, that was me.

I'd finally mustered up the courage to define what we were, laid my heart out there, and explained my love, really thinking I was going to hear that the feelings were reciprocated only to hear him stammer, "I don't...yeah, I don't feel the same way."

I was crushed. I hadn't dated anyone for over two years before this person came into my life, and I thought he was *The One*. He checked off all of my boxes – he just did it for me. I felt love in the way we interacted and the way he treated me. When we "made love," it didn't feel like meaningless sex. Don't clutch your pearls – yep, I was operating in ministry and still fornicating. That was an issue by itself, but I'm going to be honest with you so that you feel comfortable being honest with yourself.

He didn't have a problem spending money on me or taking me places and was always so kind and gentle – we literally never had one cross word with each other. As someone who spent most of her adult life in and out of toxic relationships, I wasn't used to that type of treatment, so for me, I thought it was mutual love and respect.

To hear, "Yeah, I don't feel the same." I couldn't wrap my head around it.

In the past, I'd always been the person who stayed in relationships too long or subjected myself to subpar treatment. Still, I'd done some inner work on myself before this relationship/non-relationship, and I had some pride, so I immediately cut everything. I stopped making phone calls, stopped any date nights, and definitely cut off sex. If someone could be with me for almost a year and not have any feelings, I wasn't going to give them access to my brain or body.

The next day after the breakup, I cried out to God and said, "Papa, what do I do? I can't go through another heartbreak. I won't survive it." He very plainly spoke to me and said, *"Pursue ME, and let him pursue you."*

Psalm 91 says, *He that dwelleth in the secret place of the Most High Shall abide **under** the shadow of the Almighty.* To *dwell* is to live or reside in a place. In this case, it's the secret place of God. The place where

He will reveal His thoughts toward you, show you your worth, and the plans He has for you.

Under the shadow of the Almighty God, you may find yourself in isolation while you learn to hear God's voice and He makes himself large in your life. You will learn to rest in God and cast your cares, fears, and hurt on Him.

When you abide (remain, stay) under the shadows, you will find this is the place where your pain meets purpose. You'll experience joy as an anecdote for your depression. Your productivity will increase, you will find that your creativity will be at an all-time high, and where you thought you wouldn't be able to survive one day, you'll find yourself *thriving* six months later.

That year, my business hit six figures for the first time, I launched my first retreat and began empowering women worldwide. My influence increased, and I began traveling and preaching. Even though the tangible evidence of obedience to God was amazing, my relationship with Him was most important. I had never experienced love like His, and for the first time, I began to truly love myself.

I won't lie to you; at first, it wasn't easy. I was lonely again, and I hated it. Even while I pursued God, I hurt. I cried for months, pursued God, and learned to hear his voice. I cried and followed God's voice, and He produced greatness in my life. I began to let my purpose overshadow my pain; not only did He heal my heart, but God received the glory out of my life.

People often advise, "The fastest way to get over a man is to get under a new one." Yep, I was told that, and if I may be candid with you, I think this is one of the dumbest and most ineffective ways to move on from a relationship. This may be effective in distracting you from the person who hurt you, but only for a moment; it does nothing to heal your heart.

The fastest way to get over a man is to get under THE MAN (God), who is willing and more than capable of giving you everything you desire and need. He will heal your heart and establish you on the right path for your life (Psalm 37:23).

I invite you to abide. Bury yourself so deep in God that the next man who enters your life has to go to God to find you. Everything you want is on the other side of *who* you pursue.

A Prayer of Forgiveness & Trust
Based on Psalm 91
(Pray audibly, even if it is a whisper)

Lord, I ask you that you forgive me for every time I've stepped in front of you, did not obey your instructions, and willfully moved outside of the safety of your righteousness.

As I fall deeper in love with you, I trust that the man you have for me will seek and find me in your secret place. The place where I choose to dwell and remain hidden while I am healed, protected, and prepared to be the wife you've called me to be. (Psalms 91:1,14)

Lord, you alone are my place of refuge and safety. You are my God, and I trust you. I trust you completely. (Psalm 91:2,14)

I thank you for rescuing and protecting me from the traps of toxic, abusive, or loveless relationships and the deadly disease of jealousy, envy, low self-esteem, and offense that would draw me further from you. (Psalm 91:3)

Lord Of Hosts, you promised that you would satisfy me with long life. I ask that you order your angels to protect me wherever I go as I place my complete trust in you and the power of your name. The enemy will stay under my feet as you silence his roar and divert every evil scheme he may send my way. (Psalm 91:10-16)

Even when singleness hurts and feels lonely, thank you for hiding me under your wings and shielding me until I am found by the one you desire to be the keeper of my heart. (Psalm 91:4,9,10)

Despite what I've been through, I will not be afraid of the schemes of the enemy. I trust you completely with my heart; I take refuge in you, that you are completing a good work in me and my future spouse. (Psalm 91:5,6,9)

I will allow you to process me, and help me conquer my offenses and hurt so that I will not view each person through a lens of pain. Though divorce may be all around me, my future marriage will be blessed, and the love I give will be given back to me. (Psalm 91:7,8)

____

____

____

____

____

____

____

____

____

____

____

____

____

There are gems in the word of God. Take time to study your word daily. Here is a list of scripture from within the chapter to get you started.

- Psalm 37:23
- Psalm 91
- Proverbs 3:5,6
- Joshua 1:9
- Psalm 37:3-5
- Psalm 118:8
- Mark 11:24

Lord, as I reflect on your word for my life, my thoughts are: _______________________

____

____

____

____

____

____

____

____

____

The scripture(s) that resonated with me the most:

____
____
____
____
____
____
____
____
____
____

I will apply the scripture to my life by:

____
____
____
____
____
____
____
____
____
____

Chapter Three
Heart Repair

Hey, Queen! Consider me the DEBT COLLECTOR. I'm coming for every fragmented piece of your heart for the sole purpose of making it whole again. Chile, this isn't a book about bashing men because I love a wonderful God-fearing man. **This book is about growing deeper in God, reconnecting with yourself, and allowing God to restore your heart to its full capacity so there is room to receive love again.**

I remember a few years ago; I would proudly proclaim that I hadn't had a credit card for about ten years and that I only purchased using cash. I would tell people, "If I don't have cash for it, then I don't need it." Sounds responsible, right? Yep, it sounds like real adulting. People would be so impressed, and I would beam with pride, but it wasn't the full truth.

The real reason I'd stopped using credit cards was not because I was financially mature; it was because all of my credit cards were maxed out, and I didn't have a choice. The real truth is that I was not good with money. I didn't say "no" to a purchase that didn't serve me well, I was addicted to having what I wanted when I wanted it, and I didn't protect my credit.

Fast forward about 20 years, I now have a good relationship with money, know how to handle credit, and use it only when needed. It took honesty and intention to get to this place. Just like having good financial credit requires intention, taking care of your heart does as well.

This isn't the first time I've been on a Man Fast, but this is the first time I was intentional about it. I tried to embark on a Man Fast in 2019 because, after years of abuse, my heart was maxed out. The pain my heart had endured, some of it was intentional by people in my past, and some people just weren't ready to love me correctly because of their own pain. Now that I can be completely honest with myself, I allowed a lot of it.

The real truth is that I handled my heart the same way I handled my credit – I didn't. I was not good to my heart; I didn't say "no" to relationships that didn't serve me well, and I didn't protect my heart. I also jumped into relationships without exercising the power of forgiveness, limiting my capacity to fully love and be loved. Unforgiveness also causes us to see the world through the lens of pain that we just prayed about in the last chapter.

I remember being younger, and sometimes my mother wouldn't give me a bandaid if I had a cut. Once the bleeding stopped, she would say, "It needs some air so that it can heal faster." I didn't like that because it forced me to see the open wound, and it also restricted my movement because I had to be careful.

When we are in pain, we don't make rational decisions. We lean toward the fast fix that will patch the wound and put it out of sight so that we don't see it. It's like that with our hearts. Forgiveness feels hard (at first) because it requires us to face the hurt when we would rather pretend it didn't exist.

I used to hate the word forgiveness, but we can't escape it. Matthew 6:12 lifts this prayer, *And forgive us our debts, as we forgive our debtors.* We often look at this as if it is about money being owed, but it refers to any offense that has been committed. If we want God to forgive us when we have sinned, then we *must* forgive others. This is non-negotiable as Matthew 6:14,15 solidifies it by saying, *14 For if ye forgive men their trespasses, your heavenly Father will also forgive you: 15 But if ye forgive not men their trespasses, neither will your Father forgive your trespasses.*

When people have hurt us, that is a debt owed. It is a trespass, but we must forgive and cancel that debt if we want to walk in the full freedom of God's forgiveness. This doesn't mean that you are denying the pain you've experienced because you do, in fact, have to be brave and face it. But God comforts the brokenhearted (Psalm 34:18), and if we truly trust Him with our hearts, we have to give Him the space to bring us healing with His presence (2 Corinthians 1:3-4).

Forgiveness also doesn't mean that the person gets away with how they have mishandled us. Guess what, the Lord doesn't like it when we have been done wrong, and He avenges us (Romans 12:19). How he does it is not our business. That used to be the hardest part for me, that I wouldn't necessarily know how God dealt with someone else, but the longer we focus on the other person, the longer the wound stays open. It's like picking a scab and reexposing the wound. It never properly heals and eventually leaves a scar. God desires for our hearts to be restored and free of scaring (Jeremiah 30:17).

Did you know that unforgiveness causes health issues? Chronic stress, high blood pressure, heart disease, weakened immunity, depression, and paranoid personality disorder have been linked to unforgiveness![1] In Matthew 9:2, Jesus healed a man with Palsy by forgiving his sins. The Amplified Bible reads, *They brought to Him a man who was paralyzed, lying on a stretcher. Seeing their [active] faith [springing from confidence in Him], Jesus said to the paralytic, do not be afraid, son; your sins are forgiven [the penalty is paid, the guilt removed, and you are declared to be in right standing with God].*

Some of the religious leaders were upset about Jesus' declaration, and Jesus asked, Why do you think evil is *in your hearts? 5 For which is easier, to say, 'Your sins are forgiven and the penalty paid,' or to say, 'Get up and walk'? [Both are possible for God; both are impossible for man.] 6 But so that you may know that* the Son of Man has authority *and* the power on earth to forgive sins"—then He said to the paralytic, "Get up, pick up your stretcher and go home." *(Matthew 9:4b-6 AMP).*

---

[1] The Negative Effects of Unforgiveness On Mental Health
https://www.theravive.com/today/post/the-negative-effects-of-unforgiveness-on-mental-health-0001467.aspx

Here's the reveal – the man could have got up and walked as soon as Jesus declared his sins were forgiven. Jesus knew the man with Palsy was brought to him specifically for healing because the beginning of Matthew 9:2 tells us that. Jesus *chose* to forgive his sins as a conduit for healing his physical ailment.

Jesus spoke the words of healing to prove a point to the religious teachers, but the healing had already occurred. Now, why did Jesus heal the man? He healed because He saw the faith of his friends. Their faith moved Him to action.

What does this mean for us? Forgiveness is a spoken choice of healing (we heal when we forgive). Forgiveness is *not* a feeling; it's faith-activated. Faith activates the movement of God, and He heals us through our declaration of forgiveness. I used to think that I had to *feel* forgiveness in order to walk in forgiveness. So, I pretty much would ignore the hurt of a situation until I found another man to distract me from those feelings, but they never went anywhere.

There is no power in feelings – our emotions are not reliable. All power rests in God's hands. Now, I quickly go to God and declare by faith, "Lord, I choose to forgive (insert name) for (insert offense). Please heal me from the pain of this betrayal. Right now, I still feel hurt and angry, but I don't want anything to separate me from you, so I choose to forgive, and I release (their name) into the freedom of my forgiveness. "

Pieces of Me

INSTRUCTIONS: Each puzzle piece represents a person who has a piece of your heart – *whether it was a committed relationship or not*. Write their name. It's okay if you don't fill up the heart, and if you need more space, use another sheet of paper to create a list.

Reflection

List the people from the "Pieces of Me," activity:

How do you feel looking at the pieces that are still "claimed" by another person?

What happened in the relationship(s)? Is there a pattern?

____

____

____

____

____

____

What *hurt/still hurts* about the heartbreak(s)?

____

____

____

____

____

____

What would your freedom look like/feel like if you released them to the Lord and allowed Him to take your pain?

____

____

____

____

____

____

Prayer of Forgiveness & Heart Reconciliation
(Pray audibly even if it is a whisper)

Lord, thank you for your forgiveness of all I have done. I choose to forgive myself for all I have subjected myself to. I was not good to my heart; I didn't say "no" to relationships that didn't serve me well, and I didn't protect my heart.

Lord, I *choose* to forgive (insert every name from The Pieces of Me Activity) for (insert offense). Please heal me from the pain of this betrayal. I don't want anything to separate me from you, so I choose to forgive, and I release (insert name) into the freedom of my forgiveness.

Lord, I ask that you reconcile every part of my heart. I recall each part that I freely gave away, that was stolen, and held hostage by any unforgiveness, resentment, need for revenge, anger, hate and bitterness. I place my heart fully in your hands and ask you to hold it until you deem it time to be held by the one you have prepared to be my husband.

____

____

____

____

____

____

____

There are gems in the word of God. Take time to study your word daily. Here is a list of scripture from within the chapter to get you started.

- Matthew 6:14,15
- Psalm 34:18
- 2 Corinthians 1:3-4
- Romans 12:19
- Jeremiah 30:17
- Matthew 9:2-6
- Colossians 3:13

Lord, as I reflect on your word for my life, my thoughts are: ________________________

____

____

____

____

____

____

____

____

____

____

The scripture(s) that resonated with me the most:

I will apply the scripture to my life by:

Chapter Four
Healing From Heartbreak

Here's the reality, love is addicting, and heartbreak sucks! We all experience it at some point in our life. Heartbreak causes stress, and lots of it, especially if it was an unexpected loss, it literally impacts our brain and body[2].

In going through heartbreak, I was seeking healing and answers. God had given me instruction to seek Him daily, and I was drawing closer to Him. I came across a study about how being connected to God LITERALLY changes our brain, and I wondered if heartbreak had a physical impact as well.

This Is Your Brain IN LOVE:

Scientifically, the brain releases a collection of happy hormones when we experience love: Dopamine, and

---

[2] Four Surprising Ways Heartbreak Affects Your Body
https://askdrnandi.com/heartbreak-affects-your-body

Serotonin[3]. These hormones make us feel more relaxed, stress-free, hopeful, trusting, and overall psychologically stable. As a matter of fact, love releases so much dopamine that the brain produces a euphoria associated with the use of Alcohol and Cocaine[4]. Have you been wondering why love is so hard to give up? It's addicting.

This Is Your Brain On A BREAK UP:

Because love is a "drug" to the brain, it is addicting, and losing it creates similar effects to withdrawing from a drug. Crazy right? So here's the deal, studies show that love is almost like a reward system, so when there is a breakup, that reward is taken away from the brain, and it responds by releasing **stress hormones like cortisol and epinephrine.**

When your body has too much cortisol, it sends signals to increase the blood supply to your muscles. That causes cramps, tension, headaches, chest pain, dizziness, physical exhaustion, etc.[5] So, when you feel like you are physically hurting during heartbreak, it's because you are.

So, how do you begin to heal from heartbreak? These are the steps I took to heal and move forward.

---

[3] Love, Actually: The Science Behind Lust, Attraction, and Companionship: https://sitn.hms.harvard.edu/flash/2017/love-actually-science-behind-lust-attraction-companionship/

[4] Love and the Brain: https://hms.harvard.edu/news-events/publications-archive/brain/love-brain

[5] The Pain Is Real: 8 Scientific Effects Heartbreak Has On The Body https://www.elitedaily.com/dating/scientific-reasons-why-a-broken-heart-is-really-bad-for-you

1.STOP MINIMIZING YOUR RELATIONSHIPS

The first thing we are going to stop doing is downplaying the word "relationship" and what it means. A relationship is simply a connection between two objects or, in this case, people. And people like to minimize the word because they are afraid to make a *commitment.*

It's funny because people have all sorts of names to avoid commitment, but it doesn't matter if you call it a situationship, talking, a connection – you can call it an entanglement. It still means that it is a relationship. The parameters of it should be defined, not minimized.

Everyone's threshold for a relationship is different. The amount of energy used, emotion, development of feelings, time spent, and intimacy needed to fulfill one's definition of a relationship will differ, so it is possible that you saw your connection with a person differently than the way they saw it.

I dated someone for almost a year, and our actions were that of two people in a relationship. I trusted this person; we were only seeing each other. He knew intimate details about myself, my children, and my business. I knew his private matters as well and even went house hunting with him. I catered to him as a partner; he had access to my body and my finances; we spent a lot of time together, only for me to find out that He didn't see me as anything more than a friend.

For a long time after that, I walked around, embarrassed that I had been in a relationship with someone who wasn't in a relationship with me. That's the way I defined the breakup. I used to say, "I don't know what we were. I loved him, but he didn't love me back."

I made three mistakes here. The first is that I never set any boundaries. If I would have had boundaries, I wouldn't have given him relationship benefits without a commitment. The second mistake is that I pressed for a commitment and continued with what was relationship behavior (on my part) when I didn't get one. Thirdly, allowing him to solely define/not define what we were left me in a state of hurt and confusion when it was over.

One day, I woke up and spoke a hard truth to myself, "This *was* a relationship, but it didn't serve me well. He didn't claim me, and I freely gave of myself anyway. I won't ever allow myself to be in a one-sided relationship again."

We're talking about how to heal from heartbreak. You have to be honest with yourself about how you see things. If it was a relationship to you, admit it to yourself so you can learn, grow, and *glow* forward.

When you look at the relationship(s) that have shaped where you are at this very moment, what is the hard truth? ___________________________

____

____

____

____

<u>2. DON'T BE ASHAMED OF LOVING SOMEONE; INCREASE YOUR REQUIREMENTS FOR SHARING IT.</u>

Ever felt and/or called yourself "stupid" for loving the way you do? I used to feel the same way until the Lord spoke to me and said, *"You were created to love; it sets you apart. I handcrafted you to have that big heart."*

One cold November night in 2021, the Lord had a beautiful poetic conversation with me that I put into a book, "The Bodyguard Of My Heart." This is one of the lines from that conversation. I sobbed into my pillow when the Lord spoke these words to me. I *wasn't* stupid for loving the way I do – I was created to do that, and so were you.

Don't be ashamed of the why or how you loved someone; next time, be more selective about whom you release it to. Our love is precious and valuable; it should be earned.

What does it look like when you love someone?

____

____

____

What makes the way you love special? (It's okay to brag about yourself)

____

____

____

<u>3. ACCEPT WHAT *IS* AND RELEASE WHAT *ISN'T*</u>

If you truly want to heal, you must *accept what is and release what isn't*. For example, I was very much in love with someone for years. I saw him as my forever love and not only wanted to be in a relationship, but eventually, I hoped that we would be married. He didn't feel the same, and even though we immediately parted ways, I held onto hope for yearsssss that he would "come to his senses." If another man had come along, my heart wouldn't have even been open to the possibility.

Part of my Man Fast required me to face the hard truth that I had locked myself away for someone who knew he had the key to my heart and refused to use it. When God led me through this process and said, **"*Accept what is, release what isn't*."**

I had to tell myself, "I accept that I am single right now. I release the idea that _________ is coming back. He has had enough time, and I will not wait for someone who isn't sure about me."

This wasn't easy for me to do; it hurt, and initially, I was embarrassed that I had put my heart on lockdown. But I then became my ow best friend and encouraged myself, "You're about to experience meeting the love of your life- *YOU*. Until God sends someone to love you as He does, start by loving yourself like your life depends on it."

I want you to take some time to do the same thing.

What hard truth(s) do you need to <u>accept</u> right now?"

____

____

____

____

____

____

____

What do you need to <u>release</u> to move forward?"

____

____

____

____

____

____

____

How will you begin loving yourself more?

____

____

____

____

____

____

____

5. *FEEL* THE FEELS.

Sometimes, the healing process hurts worse than the wound itself. This is why we try to avoid feeling anything at all but to truly heal; you need to honor your feelings – feel the feels. Just don't get stuck there and continue to move forward. It doesn't matter how hurt you are, life continues, and you should too.

You can give yourself a few days to completely wallow in your feelings, but get up on the third day – I mean, even Jesus rose on the third day, didn't he? (A little humor; I hope it made you smile. If it didn't, it will eventually). After that, I like to put time limits on my moments. I'll literally tell myself, "Tamika, you have 10 minutes to feel this, then we are moving forward!" Yes, I talk to myself in the third person; it helps.

In whatever timeframe I give myself, I am intentional about identifying *how* I really feel, *why* I feel that way, and if there is anything that can be done about it. We feel more than just happiness, sadness, and anger, even though those are usually the easiest to recognize.

For example, I remember that about nine months after my divorce, I was understandably still healing from it. One evening, I thought about the fact that I wasn't married anymore. I felt miserable and like a failure. This wasn't the first time I'd felt this way, and normally, I would fall into days of depression behind it. This time, I chose to do something different and gave myself fifteen minutes to *feel the feels*.

During those 15 minutes, I self-corrected. I really thought about where I was emotionally. I *wasn't* miserable – I was actually proud of myself for fighting for my freedom, moving into my own place, and taking care of my children.

No, I *wasn't* miserable. After some thought, I landed on disappointment. I was disappointed that things weren't going the way I'd hoped. Money was really tight, and I didn't feel successful in the school I was teaching at – but I was still making it on my own. For that, I was proud. I wasn't a failure.

See how drastically different the initial emotions were compared to what they ended up being? You can do this too. From now on, I want you to give yourself permission to **Feel the Feels, set a time for feeling them, identify the emotion, then intentionally pick yourself up and move forward**.

Emotions Wheel

Use the Emotion Wheel below identify difficult feelings. There is also corresponding scripture for you to read.

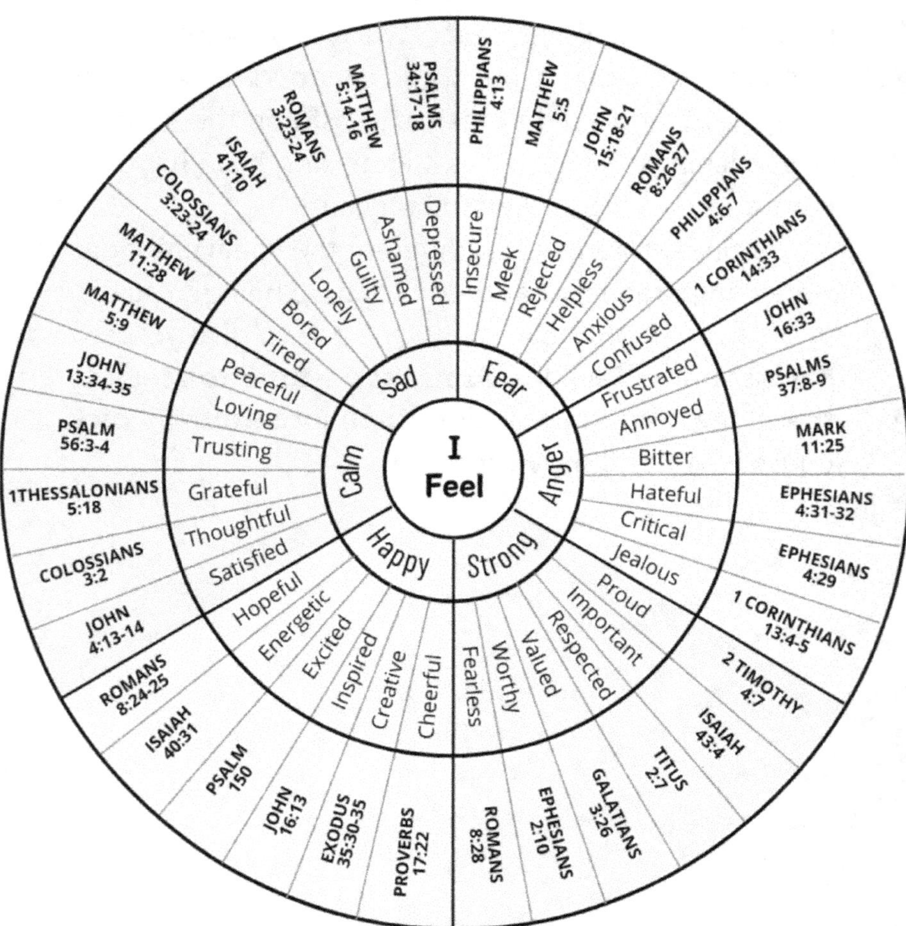

During your time of refection consider the following:

- Right now, I feel (Identify emotion)___________
- I am giving myself _________ minutes to *feel the feels.*
- I feel this way because_________________
- I *choose* to move forward by___________

Prayer For A Healed Heart & Emotional Stability
(Pray audibly, even if it is a whisper)

Father, thank you for reconciling the fragmented pieces of my heart. Today, I come to you and ask you to divinely heal my heart from the trauma of toxic relationships, abusive connections, and learned behavior that has pulled me from the destiny you have set before me.

Abba Father, I ask that you quickly restore the time that has been held up by destructive heart decisions. May my desires line up with your will for my life that not only will I live a fulfilled life, but that I may be vessel to help others.

Father, I ask that you bring emotional stability to my life that I may be free to walk in and receive the love that you have for me. Please remove all memory recall of emotional trauma I have experienced from my heart, mind, and entire body that I might walk in complete freedom and perfect peace.

____

____

____

____

____

There are gems in the word of God. Take time to study your word daily. Here is a list of scripture from within the chapter to get you started.

- Psalm 34:18
- Psalm 147:3
- Isaiah 61:1
- Matthew 11:28-30
- 1 Peter 5:7
- 1 Corinthians 13
- Jeremiah 29:11

Lord, as I reflect on your word for my life, my thoughts are: _______________________

____

____

____

____

____

____

____

____

____

The scripture(s) that resonated with me the most:

____
____
____
____
____
____
____
____
____
____
____

I will apply the scripture to my life by:

____
____
____
____
____
____
____
____
____

PART II

Reclaiming My Identity

Chapter Five
All Things New

17 Therefore if any man be in Christ, he is a new creature: old things are passed away; behold, all things become new.
2 Corinthians 5:17

There is beauty in starting over, beginning with a clean slate, and possibly reinventing yourself. There is no reason why you have to remain the way you've always been. I've been married and divorced twice. In 2019, I felt unworthy and like tainted goods sitting in the aftermath of my second failed marriage. Surely, no one would want me, right?

In Christ, we are new creatures – we are able to become new as many times as we need to. We can shed our "old man" and walk into newness. Once I grasped this concept, I stopped looking at myself as "tainted goods," I became excited to meet the best version of me waiting for me on the other side of my process.

In getting to the best version of *you*, let's take a moment and examine what may be holding you back from actually taking the leap to start over.

I've Put Too Much Time In This Relationship
Oftentimes, we don't like to move on from relationships because of the time we've put into them. 2 Corinthians 10:5b gives us instruction to *Take every thought captive and make it obedient to Christ.* Why? Well, part of the reason is that most of our decisions come from an emotional place that starts with a thought.

For example, nothing would make me more nauseous than the thought of someone else reaping the benefits of my *labor* – the time and energy I'd put into the relationship. So, the idea of staying in a relationship that didn't serve me well was more appealing than starting over.

I had a skewed vision of what a profitable investment was. A profitable investment is one where there is a return on investment (ROI); otherwise, you are left with a loss. How much of yourself have you lost in shackling yourself to empty relationships?

I Don't Want to Be Alone
Have you ever enjoyed a night watching television by yourself? This is an example of being *alone.* On the other hand, have you felt sad because you didn't have the company of other people watching television with you? Well, this describes the feeling of *loneliness.*

It's important to recognize the difference between being alone and feeling lonely. We use these words interchangeably, but they are different. Many of us don't want to start over because we don't like feeling *lonely,* but being alone doesn't automatically equate to feeling lonely.

Now, I'll be honest, in the beginning, it was hard for me to be alone. I was used to being consumed by thoughts of someone else: how do I make him happy? How do I not make him upset today? Why didn't he call me today? How does he really feel about me? When will I see him again?

Sheesh, that line of questioning will drive anyone crazy and cause stress! How did I ever do it? I'll tell you how – I liked the feeling of *belonging* to someone, even though I didn't like the treatment.

As you begin to put yourself first and rediscover the things you like and dislike, you'll start to enjoy your own company. You will be busy walking in purpose. There is nothing more satisfying than flowing in the reason why you were created.

Eventually, *being* alone won't *feel* lonely. It will just be a state of being versus an emotion.

Will Anyone Else Want Me?

The short answer is YES! You're amazing; why wouldn't someone else want to be with you? I have found that the things we are insecure about aren't as prevalent to others as we think. Physically, I used to be very insecure about my dark complexion, my slim shape because I wasn't blessed with the larger "black girl booty," as well as my crooked teeth.

Gurlllll (I meant to spell it that way), when I allowed God to pour into me about how He sees me – I've never felt more beautiful. Those things don't matter, and the glory of God resting on me is a magnet for suitors. Healing is the new sexy. Nothing is more attractive than a confident woman walking in healing and purpose. Of course, someone else will want you! Now go ahead and heal!

Some Hard Truths of Starting Over

It's time to face some hard truths about starting over and it's when we have to look in the mirror. A few years ago, I had a friend who dropped a bomb on me. She told me that we date a mirror version of ourselves. I realized it was accurate when I ran through a mental list of the people I had allowed in my life. And at that particular moment in my life, I was able to honestly say that I was insecure, attention-seeking, felt unworthy, broken, and lonely. When I looked at the people I was entertaining, they looked the same way.

Some of the people that I allowed in my life at the time were a drug dealer who I later found out was married. Also, a person who had pursued me for years only to continually ghost me after I gave him a chance, as well as a person who attempted to pimp me out. That's a whole 'nother book, lol.

Then, two years later, after going to therapy and doing some inner work, I decided that I was ready to jump back into the dating pool. By this point, I *knew* that I was worthy of love. I didn't think that I had any more brokenness, and I had learned to enjoy my own company, but in all honesty, I was still in a place of loneliness and insecurity, and guess what? I attracted someone that I thought was amazing, but they still dealt with major insecurities from prior relationships just like I did.

Because of my insecurities, I didn't have boundaries. I hadn't even considered what my boundaries would be. Truthfully, I was afraid to have them, afraid of being alone anymore. So this was a relationship or a situation where I thought I was in a relationship with someone who was not in a relationship with me, and I ultimately was left broken. Again.

That brokenness... taking the time to look at myself in the mirror and see the relationship that I had invited into my life... *That* brokenness made me give it all up to God and ask Him what to do. You see, that type of brokenness is the kind that feels suffocating. You can't breathe. Your heart hurts that much. And so, I went to Papa... That's my name for God, and He told me to pursue HIM and let him pursue me.

Initially, I thought I knew who the "him" Papa was talking about, but as I began building a relationship with Him, I stopped focusing on who the "him" would be. I realized that at the right time, God would connect me with the person who has the capacity to hold all of who I am. We would be a reflection of each other. I became more and more excited with the understanding that if God was working on me, then surely, He was working on whomever *he* was. Whew, what a beautiful relationship it is going to be!

Are You What You Want In A Mate?
This isn't always a popular question, but it's necessary to ask. Are you what you want? After I was divorced, I remember saying, "The next man that gets with me needs to have a good credit score, his own car, home, and he can't be broke! I can't do broke men anymore."

"Are you those things?" Papa asked me.

Why did Papa have to play me like that? God will put you in your place, won't He?

I took a serious look at myself...again...I was living with my parents and was afraid to move on my own. My credit score was 516, and my bank account had a negative balance. Yep, I had no right to demand anything from another person.

My desire shifted from *finding a man* to fulfill my list to *becoming a woman worthy* of being *found* by that type of man. Within a month of that revelation, I changed jobs, prepared to move to another state completely, and started working with a credit counselor. If I wanted something different, I had to be different.

Someone will be upset that I said, "A woman *worthy* of being found by that type of man." The word "worthy" means to be deserving. Listen, if God loves you so much that He's preparing the man who is worthy/deserving of being loved by you, don't you think He wants the same for His son? Sure, He does.

Don't be offended. As you come to the full understanding of how valuable you are, you won't settle for less than you deserve. Neither will your future husband. God is completing the work.

Starting over doesn't have to be negative. God makes all things new. Will the process always feel good? No, but you don't feel good where you are right now. Pick your "pain." Will you pick the pain of the process which you know will eventually end in your favor? Or will you *stay* in the state that you're in and simply hope for the best?

Reflection

How much of yourself have you lost in shackling yourself to empty relationships?

____
____
____
____
____
____

What is holding you back from starting over?

____
____
____
____
____
____

What are the benefits of starting over?

____
____
____
____
____
____

What do you want in a mate?

____

____

____

____

____

____

____

____

What do you need to work on to be a reflection of all that you want?

____

____

____

____

____

____

____

____

Prayer For A Restored Identity In Christ
(Pray audibly, even if it is a whisper)

Lord, please forgive me for rooting my identity in a relationship(s) when it should be rooted in You. I ask that you reconcile all fragmented pieces of my identity back to you. May I be put back together and used by you as you initially intended when you created me.

By faith, I am saved and have full access to all benefits of salvation through Christ Jesus. Lord, please help me to fix my gaze on things above (Colossians 3:1-4). I believe that Christ loves me, died for me, and now lives in me (Galatians 2:20). That display of love makes me worthy of a pure and unselfish love, one where I will be loved as Christ loves the church (Ephesians 5:25).

Lord, I choose to begin again, this time with you in control. I rebuke the spirits of fear, loneliness, abandonment, and depression that I would try to keep in a space of stagnation instead of moving forward as a new creature.

There are gems in the word of God. Take time to study your word daily. Here is a list of scripture from within the chapter to get you started.

- 2 Corinthians 5:17
- 2 Corinthians 10:5
- Colossians 3:1-4
- Galatians 2:20
- Ephesians 5:25
- Colossians 2:9-10
- Jeremiah 1:5

Lord, as I reflect on your word for my life, my thoughts are: _______________________________

____

____

____

____

____

____

____

____

____

____

The scripture(s) that resonated with me the most:

____
____
____
____
____
____
____
____
____
____

I will apply the scripture to my life by:

____
____
____
____
____
____
____
____
____
____

Chapter Six

Are You Addicted To The Pain?

'm addicted to the high I get from making other people happy."

That's the first thing I said to my therapist. I'd written that in the notes section of my phone that morning. This was the first time I'd ever worked with a therapist. My second marriage was coming to an end, and my life was spinning out of control. At the time, I worked for the school system, and I was given six free sessions.

I was a people pleaser; this was the first time I'd admitted it. I was embarrassed and relieved at the same time. Embarrassed when I thought about all I'd subjected myself to to have someone in my life – lovers, friends, church affiliation, clients...I gave too much of myself to everyone. I hated it. It was overwhelming, but I loved it when I heard the pitch change to happiness in someone's voice or saw their smile—that split second validated me. It added value to my life.

In one of my sessions, the therapist, Dr. V, asked me to tell her about my past relationships — there weren't many; I married young and spent much of my adult years as someone's wife. Every single relationship I'd *ever* been in shared the same ingredients – the same type of childhood and relationship traits, and ultimately treated me the same way.

"You like feeling needed," the therapist responded matter-of-factly, biting on the arm of her glasses after I recounted each relationship.

"Whew!" My head snapped like someone had slapped me. "You're absolutely right, Dr. V!"

I ended up in the same type of relationship because of my appetite; I craved relationships because they validated me. I am a natural giver, but instead of understanding that there are levels to giving and receiving, I always I tried to "save" the other person.

In the previous chapter, we looked at ways to heal from heartbreak. We discovered that love produces a euphoria similar to that of alcohol or cocaine use because it releases Dopamine. Dopamine causes you to want, desire, seek out, and search[6]. This means that pretty much anything you desire, seek out, and acquire will release the addicting hormone from eating foods you crave, exercising, having sex, people-pleasing, and more.

What is your drug? What is the toxic thing you subject yourself to in order to feel seen, worthy, accepted…loved? For me, it was people-pleasing. It carried over to all facets of my life, from romantic relationships, work relationships, church, etc. I would do almost anything to get the high.

---

[6] https://www.psychologytoday.com/us/basics/dopamine

When it came to men, there was almost no limit. I gave my body, brains, money, and time. I subjected myself to abuse and used my body as currency. When a man didn't give me enough attention, I responded sexually, from pictures, videos, and the act itself. I wanted attention – needed attention like the air I breathed.

The thing about neediness that no one talks about is that it has a stench. You don't need to say that you're needy – it carries an odor that will repel men who are looking for someone of value and draw men who wish to prey on your insecurities.

Some years ago, I was so needy that one of the men who claimed to love me attempted to pimp me out—tried to get me to dance at a strip club and dance for one of his friend's bachelor parties. He even talked to me about how easy it would be for me to attract and entertain older white men.

"You have a great set of knockers (breasts), and you can dance; you could make an easy $1500 to $3000 a night."

First of all, can we both take a moment to share in an eye roll and disgusted sigh? "Knockers?" That's corny; who calls breasts knockers anymore? I should have run far, far away for so many reasons...but I was NEEDY. I couldn't wrap my head around his willingness to share me, but instead of expressing that, my self-esteem was so low that I asked, "You would still love me if I did that? Let other men see me and touch me?"

"I would love you more," was his response.

He offered to sit in the back of the club and wait outside of the homes to protect me if I chose to do it. *How sweet.* (I'm being sarcastic.)

He said he was trying to help me earn some money for my kids and me. The reality is that this was someone I was sleeping with, driving across three states to see each time we met up and sowing financially into his dreams when I had it. If he cared about me, he would have poured back into me the same way I poured. But I was needy, without boundaries, and with little pride. I wanted to be wanted.

I never went through with it. I wasn't fully living right, but I've always loved God. I was known in ministry, ran an award-winning radio station, and my parents were well-known in ministry – I couldn't do that and risk someone seeing me. Yes, that was the only thing that kept me from doing it. It wasn't my own self-respect. Remember, sex and men were my drugs – I would have done almost anything to keep them.

Whew! Those were some dark moments in my life. I used to be ashamed, but Romans 8:1 AMP (Amplified Bible) *Therefore, there is now no condemnation [no guilty verdict, no punishment] for those who are in Christ Jesus [who believe in Him as personal Lord and Savior].*

You have to believe this; once you repent and turn away from wrongdoing, there is no condemnation – no guilty verdict.

Detoxing from Toxicity

1. **Recognize that you have a "drug" addiction.** Once you admit that you have a problem, you can begin working on ways to overcome it.

   ♥ **What is your "addiction?"** ______________
   ____
   ____
   ____

2. **Take responsibility for your part.** Taking responsibility for what you have allowed doesn't absolve others for how they have treated you or made you feel. Part of the detox process is to recognize the part you've played in your own pain so that it doesn't happen again.

   ♥ **What part did you play in your own pain?**
   ____
   ____
   ____
   ____

3. **Repent and Turn Away from the wrongdoing** (Acts 3:19). This chapter focused on my drug of choice – sex, which may not be yours, but if what you lean toward is toxic, repent for that.

4. **Identify Your Triggers.** What triggers you to fall into addictive behavior? For example, one of

my triggers is when I'm stressed out or overwhelmed; my outlet used to be sex. Now, when I feel either of those, I will spend time with my family and/or friends. I don't allow myself to be alone. Now, I'm pretty good at controlling myself, but I don't test myself—that's unnecessary stress.

♥ **What triggers you to fall into addictive behavior?** _______________________

____

____

____

5. **Establish boundaries for yourself.** Don't tempt yourself. You know what triggers you and draws you in. Don't allow yourself to be in those environments, and don't permit others to cross those lines, either.

♥ What boundaries will you set for yourself to prevent you from giving in to your triggers?

____

____

____

____

6. **Spend time with God and Seek Validation From God (Matthew 6:33).** It makes sense that one of the benefits God said He was granting me through this Man Fast was that I would learn

to seek validation from Him because my destructive behaviors came from trying to be accepted, seen, loved, and validated. *Matthew 6:33 But seek ye first the kingdom of God, and his righteousness; and all these things shall be added unto you.*

Queen, I want to encourage you. Your drug of choice *today* doesn't have to control your heart, emotions, mental state, and actions of tomorrow or any other day, for that matter.

YOU ARE WORTHY. Don't allow shame and embarrassment to hold you back from your healing. I've chosen to be totally transparent so that you can be that way with yourself. If you've done things you aren't proud of, maybe you've been forced to do things, whether it was a byproduct of your own choices or not, know that God STILL LOVES YOU, and you are STILL worthy.

Prayer To Break Relationship Addictions & Ungodly Attachments
(Pray audibly, even if it is a whisper)

Lord, I ask that you forgive me for making an idol of my relationships. Please forgive me for choosing sin instead of righteous living. I ask that you forgive me for coming into agreement with addiction and choosing to live with ungodly attachments.

Father, I ask that you destroy the stronghold of every addiction, addictive, and co-dependent personality. I cast out and rebuke any and all spirits of relationship addiction, including but not limited to: Substance abuse (alcohol, illegal drugs, prescription drugs), anger, anxiety, rage, co-dependency, compulsive behavior, condemnation, cursing, depression, fear, hopelessness, impaired judgment, instability, lust, nicotine, overeating, paranoia, pornography, rebellion, shame, torment, witchcraft[7].

Father, I please sever any cord connecting me to ungodly attachments that feeds me lies and deception. Reconnect me back to you where there is fullness of joy.

---

[7] Tucker, Bev, Setting the Captives Free: Deliverance Manual, Page 26-27

There are gems in the word of God. Take time to study your word daily. Here is a list of scripture from within the chapter to get you started.

- Romans 8:1
- Acts 3:19
- Matthew 6:33
- 2 Corinthians 6:14
- Matthew 5:44
- Luke 6:28
- Psalm 147:3

Lord, as I reflect on your word for my life, my thoughts are: _______________________________

____

____

____

____

____

____

____

____

____

____

The scripture(s) that resonated with me the most:

I will apply the scripture to my life by:

PART III

Reclaiming My Body

1 Corinthians 6:19-20 (ESV), he asks, "Or do you not know that your body is a temple of the Holy Spirit within you, whom you have from God? You are not your own, for you were bought with a price. So glorify God in your body."

Chapter Seven

Let's Talk About Sex!

et's tackle this subject right now because, on the surface, this can be the hardest piece to live without. When I gave God my complete "yes," I immediately laid this before Him. Keeping myself has not always been easy for me, and honestly, I wasn't sure if I could do it.

For me, sex was not just an act of pleasure; it always got me into trouble because it clouded my judgment and created phantom feelings for people. Phantom feelings – you know what I'm talking about – you find yourself confused about a person that just the day before you weren't even thinking about them. You find yourself thinking you love a person just because you had sex with them (whether the sex was good or not).

Truth be told, in the past, I've essentially lost my mind after sex, not only surrendering my body and heart but even my money, use of my car, home, etc. To this day, I refuse to calculate the amount of money I've given to men after falling for them *after* sex. I don't want to pass out, lol!

Ever heard the term "ball and chain" to refer to marriage? If not, it's a slang term meaning "wife." The reference comes from presuming that a man's wife holds him back from doing the things he really wants to do. The origin refers to an actual ball and chain, which was a heavy metal ball secured to a prisoner's leg.[8]

Personally, I've never liked the term. I think it's silly and disrespectful; however, it's a good depiction of what sex does to a person – especially outside of marriage. Sex is often used as a distraction from the pain of heartbreak, but it's also the "binding agent" to people.

It's the Soullllll Train!

Ok, I get it; the reference to Soul Train, the television show, may be corny, but I couldn't help myself. I totally just aged myself – let's move on from that. Let's talk Soul Ties.

Relationships, intimate relationships, establish a spiritual connection, or Soul Tie. To be clear, intimacy doesn't always mean romantic.

An intimate connection simply means there is a close, personal, familiar, or private relationship with someone. We can have these types of connections with family members, friends, co-workers, etc. The Bible speaks of a close friendship between David and Jonathan in 1 Samuel 18:1 KJV, *The soul of Jonathan was knit with the soul of David, and Jonathan loved him as his own soul.*

---

[8] Ball and Chain Origin,
https://www.phrases.org.uk/meanings/54950.html

This demonstrates that there is a possibility of Soul Ties forming in non-romantic relationships, but for this book, we are speaking romantically. Suppose we are to look at this scripture and its depiction of two souls being knitted together – loving another as his or her own soul. It's becoming one with another. That is some type of bond, isn't it?

When two souls knit together, there is a *spiritual* imprint or residue that remains. This is why you can hear a certain song, smell a familiar scent, or see a person, and there is something deep within that leaps. All of a sudden, you find yourself experiencing feelings and physical reactions that you can't identify.

When we talk about reclaiming our bodies, it's important first to understand what happens when we <u>illegally</u> give our bodies away. In Numbers 22-24, we encounter a wicked prophet named Balaam, employed by the king of Moab, King Balak, to curse the Israelites in exchange for a reward. Balaam agreed to do so but said he needed God's permission to do so. Balaam attempted to curse the Israelites three different times; each time, God required him to speak a blessing over them.

Determined to get his reward, Balaam devised a plan to make the Israelites curse themselves. Can you guess what he did? Balaam advised the Moabites on how to entice the people of Israel with prostitutes and idolatry. He could not curse Israel directly, so he came up with a plan for Israel to bring a curse upon themselves. Balak followed Balaam's advice, and Israel fell into sin by worshiping Baal of Peor and committing fornication with Midianite women (Numbers 25:1-2)[9].

As a result, the people of Israel were plagued and 24,000 men died. Why? Numbers 25:3 tells us *So Israel **yoked himself** to Baal of Peor. And the anger of the LORD was kindled against Israel.* The result of sexual sin was a yoke, a covenant to Baal, a fertility god who was believed to enable the earth to produce crops and people to produce children. Baal worship was rooted in sex and involved ritualistic prostitution in the temples.

What does this mean for us? It means that righteous living grants us full access to the blessings and protection of God, and sexual sin causes us to curse ourselves. Sexual sin yokes us to the spirit of perversion and gives Satan the legal right to attack us (Numbers 25:3).

Sex in itself is not bad; after all, it was created by God as a gift for husband and wife to be fulfilling as a means of having children (Genesis 1:28), but also as a way to unify the two physically, emotionally, and spiritually (Genesis 2:18, 23–24; Matthew 19:4–6; 1 Corinthians 7:32–34).

1 Corinthians 6:16-20 gives an eye-opening depiction of what takes place when sex occurs outside of marriage.

---

[9] What was Baal of Peor in the Bible?
https://www.gotquestions.org/Baal-Peor.html

> **1 Corinthians 6:16-20 The Message Bible says,**
> *16-20 There's more to sex than mere skin on skin. Sex is as much spiritual mystery as physical fact. As written in Scripture, "The two become one." Since we want to become spiritually one with the Master, we must not pursue the kind of sex that avoids commitment and intimacy, leaving us more lonely than ever—the kind of sex that can never "become one." There is a sense in which sexual sins are different from all others. In sexual sin we violate the sacredness of our own bodies, these bodies that were made for God-given and God-modeled love, for "becoming one" with another. Or didn't you realize that your body is a sacred place, the place of the Holy Spirit? Don't you see that you can't live however you please, squandering what God paid such a high price for? The physical part of you is not some piece of property belonging to the spiritual part of you. God owns the whole works. So let people see God in and through your body.*

There is much to learn from this scripture. Let's dive in:

1. **Sex is just as much spiritual as it is physical.**
   Our bodies are here on earth, but our desire is to be spiritually connected with our Father in Heaven. Marriage is an earthly representation of how we are joined to God in the spirit. In a marriage, sexual sin destroys the relationship between husband and wife. Spiritually, our sexual sin destroys our relationship with the Father.

2. **Sexual Sin disconnects us from God.**
    1 Corinthians 3:16-17 KJV says [16]Know ye not that ye are the temple of God, and that the Spirit of God dwelleth in you? [17]If any man defile the temple of God, him shall God destroy; for the temple of God is holy, which temple ye are.

    God WILL NOT dwell in an unclean temple. That means that if you commit sexual sin, you are left uncovered. I never want to be without God, even for a few minutes of pleasure. It isn't worth it.

3. **We violate the sacredness of our bodies when we engage in sexual sin.** Wow, did you realize that your body is sacred, and it's seen that way in the eyes of God? Everyone does not have the right or deserve to touch and know your body because it is sacred. Our body is a home for Holy Spirit to dwell.

4. **God owns the whole works.**
    Our entire being – spirit and flesh belong to God. He wants all of us, not just pieces. We are representatives of God – and people should be able to experience Him with our entire beings.

1. What are your thoughts about sex being *both* spiritual and physical?

____

____

____

2. How do you view your body now that you know God considers it to be a sacred place for Holy Spirit to dwell?

____

____

____

3. Satan knows our weaknesses and intentionally sets us up to fall sexually. What are your weaknesses?

____

____

____

4. What else has God revealed to you while reading this chapter?

____

____

____

Prayer To Release Sexual Sin & Body Reconciliation
(Pray audibly, even if it is a whisper)

Lord, I ask that you forgive me for defiling my body outside of the sanctity of marriage. I ask that you forgive me for (name sexual sin you have engaged in). I renounce all pleasure associated with these sexual sins and the spirit of perversion.

I break all curses and ungodly covenants I established with any person I have been involved with.

Lord, I ask that you purify me, make me new, and heal my body, mind, memories, and emotions from the imprint of sexual perversion[10].

Father, I ask that my body, mind, soul, and spirit be reconciled to you. That when you connect me with my future mate there will be no residue of past relationships left.

____

____

____

____

____

____

---

[10] Tucker, Bev, Setting the Captives Free: Deliverance Manual, Page 18

There are gems in the word of God. Take time to study your word daily. Here is a list of scripture from within the chapter to get you started.

- 1 Corinthians 6:19-20
- 1 Samuel 18:1
- Numbers 22-24
- Numbers 25:1-3
- Genesis 1:28
- Genesis 2:18, 23–24
- Matthew 19:4–6
- 1 Corinthians 7:32–34
- 1 Corinthians 6:16-20

Lord, as I reflect on your word for my life, my thoughts are: _______________________________

____

____

____

____

____

____

____

____

The scripture(s) that resonated with me the most:

____
____
____
____
____
____
____
____
____
____

I will apply the scripture to my life by:

____
____
____
____
____
____
____
____
____

Chapter Eight
Your Worth Is Not Between Your Legs

In writing this chapter, the Lord had me go through four years of saved Snaps on my Snapchat account. I came across pictures and videos I thought I'd deleted and forgotten about. These pictures were taken months after going through my second divorce. I was shattered and cared little about *my* life. I loved my children and chose to *survive* for them.

There was a period of time when I used to engage in nasty conversations, and I used sexting – sexual text messages including nude/semi-nude photos and videos, to connect, "hook" a person, and "keep them interested." Well...that's what I *thought* it did, but ultimately, I realized it cheapened me. It's a tough lesson to learn when you find out that a person you trusted shared your pictures and videos with another person/people.

The Enemy will have you convinced that your worth lies between your legs, and you will find that sex consumes your life. It will be how you feel validated, and you will constantly think of ways to "up your game." You will put all of your worth on how well you perform sexually. Before long, the Enemy will send people your way to push your boundaries. You will find yourself doing things you never dreamed of to *feel seen and loved when,* in reality, you are being *overlooked and used.*

Ever had sex with someone who didn't look at you – they looked past you? *Overlooked and used.* You can try to convince yourself that it is something else, but you know when someone is with you but not really there. The reality is that sex will never keep a man with you. If he doesn't love you or want to be with you, he won't stay.

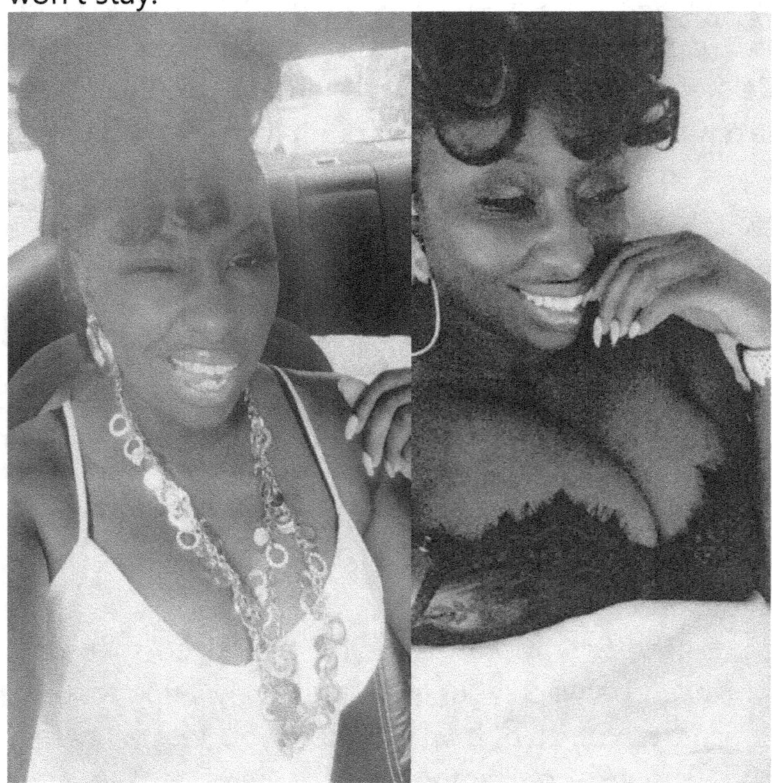

The pictures you're looking at were taken the day that I met up with a man who convinced me that he loved me so much he wanted me to have sex with him and another man that I didn't even know. I wanted to be loved, and I really tried to convince myself that because he had a large sexual appetite, this was part of his "love language."

The sad part about this is that we weren't even dating because he was *still* married! I didn't owe him anything, certainly not my body nor the need to fulfill his sexual desires. But I was broken and believed the lies the Enemy told me. The Enemy told me that:

- I had been married most of my adult life, and I deserved to do what I wanted to do. ***LIE!***
- So many people had used me in my past; at least this way, I controlled the situation. ***LIE!***
- I needed to accept the first man who showed interest in me because no one would want me after being married twice with two children. ***LIE!***
- God didn't love me anymore because of sexual sins I had already committed – this wouldn't be any worse, right? *LIE, LIE, LIE!*

That night was one of the most humiliating nights of my life. I was physically abused and passed around as they literally growled like animals. I could barely walk the next day, and they left me with the hotel bill. I didn't tell anyone about it. I added it to the list of lies that attacked my worth.

Sis, you deserve to be seen, loved, and cherished. A person who cares about you will never have you feeling otherwise. They will never pass you around like a garbage can for someone to dump their waste, but you must believe it and present yourself accordingly.

I didn't like being treated like a sexual object, but I carried myself as one, from the way I dressed to the way I spoke and behaved. I loved and hated the attention at the same time. The Enemy had me convinced that I *felt* beautiful when a man made a sexual comment or groped me, but I often felt dirty.

One day, years later, I asked God to show me how *He* saw me. He began to show me in the Word what He thought of me. He took me to the beginning, the book of Genesis, and He presented the reason why I was created and how I should be cared for.

Genesis 1:27;31

27 So God created man in his own image, in the image of God created he him; male and female created he them.

31 And God saw everything that he had made, and, behold, it was very good. And the evening and the morning were the sixth day.

> ### *Genesis 2:18-22*
>
> *18 And the LORD God said, It is not good that the man should be alone; I will make him an help meet for him.*
>
> *19 And out of the ground the LORD God formed every beast of the field, and every fowl of the air; and brought them unto Adam to see what he would call them: and whatsoever Adam called every living creature, that was the name thereof.*
>
> *20 And Adam gave names to all cattle, and to the fowl of the air, and to every beast of the field; but for Adam there was not found an help meet for him.*
>
> *21 And the LORD God caused a deep sleep to fall upon Adam, and he slept: and he took one of his ribs, and closed up the flesh instead thereof;*
>
> *22 And the rib, which the LORD God had taken from man, made he a woman, and brought her unto the man.*

In Genesis 1:27, the Lord demonstrates His desire to create man and woman in His image. I enjoy Genesis 2 because it gives us insight into the thoughts and actions of God during the creation of women. The woman was created because God saw that it was not good for man to be alone – before that, everything God had created in the Garden had a partner and the ability to reproduce. Adam was the only "creation" unable to do so.

So, God gave Adam the assignment to name the animals in the Garden before He put Him to sleep and *gifted* him with Eve. In other words, God had Adam prepare the home so that Eve entered a space already prepared for her.

Do you think that God gifted Adam with a woman who was unattractive and without intelligence? Of course not. Eve was a gift. Adam didn't tell God what He wanted in a woman; God gave him someone who would appeal to him of equal intelligence, morals, and physical attraction.

God required Adam to prepare the scene for Eve. She didn't enter the Garden and have sex with him in order to be chosen – she *was* the gift. As a matter of fact, if you go back to Genesis 1:31, it is after her creation that God looked at His creation and said it was *VERY good*.

As a woman, you are a fulfillment of God's divine assignment—God's imagination. God called you a *help meet*, not a sex thing.

Reflection

1. What are your thoughts about being a fulfillment of God's divine assignment?

____

____

____

____

2. Think of the ways you have allowed your body to be mishandled. Why did you allow it?

____

____

____

____

3. How will you better love and respect your body?

____

____

____

____

4. Going forward, what will you no longer allow?

____

____

____

____

5. What else has God revealed to you while reading this chapter?

____

____

____

____

Prayer To Reestablish Worth
(Pray audibly, even if it is a whisper)

Lord, I ask that you forgive me for rooting my worth in sexual sin. My identity and body have been reconciled to you, and you have broken the curses associated with past sexual sin.

Now, Lord, I ask that my worth, self-esteem, and value be reestablished. From this day forward, I release myself from the bondage of being a sex object. I divorce myself from every spirit that has married itself to me while being yoked to ungodly attachment.

Today, I declare that I am a daughter of God, a new creature, loved by the Most High God, and worthy of love.

____

____

____

____

____

____

____

There are gems in the word of God. Take time to study your word daily. Here is a list of scripture from within the chapter to get you started.

- Genesis 1:27;31
- Genesis 2:18-22
- Ecclesiastes 3:11
- Isaiah 54:5
- Psalm 149:4
- 1 Peter 5:10
- 1 Peter 2:9

Lord, as I reflect on your word for my life, my thoughts are: ___________________________

____

____

____

____

____

____

____

The scripture(s) that resonated with me the most:

I will apply the scripture to my life by:

Chapter Nine
MY BODY IS THE LORD'S!
Breaking Soul Ties & Denouncing Spiritual Spouses

A few weeks before the Lord sat me down to write this book, I had a dream. I was walking through a tomb with a salesman. The salesman wasn't alive, and I remember thinking that I had to be in Hell. It was dark and damp, dimly lit, and there was a mildew smell in the air. There were long metal gray box slots lining the walls where people assigned their ashes after they died.

In the dream, I was walking with two people from my past that I had been involved with sexually – a man and a woman. The salesman gave me a book, asked me to write my obituary, and told me to decide whom I wanted to be slotted with. I struggled with where I wanted to be placed because I didn't want to be with either one, but I wasn't given a different choice.

I woke up from that dream around 2 AM, unable to catch my breath and afraid. For one thing, I had not been with either person for quite some time, and I wasn't even thinking about them in that way. I thought

I was walking in deliverance. At this point, I was more than halfway through my man fast and had not engaged sexually with *anyone.* I wasn't even masturbating or watching pornography.

I cried out to God for nearly four hours and asked Him what the dream meant. "I don't want to miss You," I pleaded. "I haven't been doing anything. Please tell me what this means."

Around 6 AM, He spoke, "Denounce the spiritual marriage. Denounce the covenant."

At that moment, the Lord gave me the revelation of Soul Ties and the fact that we bind ourselves to more than just a person when we sleep with them. If we understand 1 Corinthians 6:16 MSG, which says that *sex is just as much spiritual as it is physical* – that implies that it joins the two with one another. Sex creates both a spiritual and physical covenant. Spiritually, we connect with one of two spirits – God or Satan.

<u>Sexually Transmitted Demons</u>

Sexual sin leaves us uncovered and opens the door to brokenness, and it is one of the most used weapons the enemy uses to steal innocence, kill identity, and destroy one's future; this is what the violation of molestation, rape, and sexual abuse does. The sexual sin we voluntarily commit does the same thing – it leaves us uncovered and broken, and we invite unnecessary warfare into our lives. This is a big deal because when we deal with evil spirits, we don't deal with them one at a time. Demons attack like a little gang – they don't come by themselves.

If we revisit 1 Corinthians 6:16 MSG, it says, *There's more to sex than mere skin on skin. Sex is as much spiritual mystery as physical fact.* Sex is a binding agent – it binds two people together both physically and spiritually. Sex was designed to shift our identity from being an *individual party of one to a partnership of oneness with our partner that is sanctioned* by God.

When we have sex outside of marriage is a gateway to bondage. Our identity is bound to the person(s) we are sleeping with and holds us in bondage. Fear, rejection, abandonment, anger, rage, inferiority, insecurity, depression, confusion, and manipulation are some of the common spirits that attach themselves. And we can't forget that this causes us to be separated from God.

Let's examine some of the gateways:

FORNICATION

We've always been taught that fornication is sex outside of marriage – and this is true, but it's bigger than that. The word *fornication* comes from the Greek term *porneia* (from which we get our English word *pornography*) and is often linked with adultery in the Bible[11]. The Hebrew translation for *fornication* and used in context with pagan idolatry and spiritual

---

[11] What does the Bible say about fornication?
https://www.gotquestions.org/Bible-fornication.html

whoredom. Much of pagan "worship" included sex in their rituals. Temple prostitutes were common in the worship of Baal and other false gods. Sexual sin of all kinds was not only accepted in these religions but encouraged as a means to greater blessings from the gods for the worshipers, particularly in the increase of their flocks and crops[12].

When I first learned that the word *fornication* was connected with idolatry, I was taken aback. I had never thought of it that way. I heard an easy-to-understand definition of it from a Prophet named Tiphani Montgomery, who said that anything we place higher than our obedience to God is an idol. Ever felt like you were a slave to sex? Like you couldn't control yourself from engaging in sex even when deep down you didn't want to or knew it wasn't good for you to do it? I remember a time in my life when I was driven by the need for sex. It wasn't just the act itself; it was everything that came with it – validation, a boost to my ego, and a false sense of control.

ADULTERY

There was a season in my life when married men flocked to me. Some tried to hide it, but most didn't. Some weren't in the church, *but* most were, and they held titles – prominent titles. They offered me money, homes, furniture for my place, and jewelry – the typical things you would expect. They didn't have a problem driving hours to see me or to pay for me to meet them

---

[12] What is the Difference Between Fornication and Adultery; https://www.gotquestions.org/fornication-adultery.html

somewhere. They also didn't have a problem taking me to public places on "dates."

I have been in church my entire life and, of course, knew that adultery is wrong, but to make myself feel better, I would say, "*He* is married, I'm not."

This was foolish talk and a lie from the enemy to keep me separated from the Lord. Here is the truth. Proverbs 6:32 NLT says, *But the man who commits adultery is an utter fool, for he destroys himself.*

Adultery means to have sex with someone other than your spouse, but to dive into the spiritual meaning, the Hebrew word "Niuph," translated as "adultery," literally means "breaking wedlock" and is also used to describe idolatrous worship[13].

Here's the thing, sex was a transaction in exchange for feeding a deeper need for companionship, someone that was easy to talk to, and someone to feed our ego and pacify our insecurities. He should have been getting that from his spouse, and I should have been going to God and allowing him to heal inner wounds to prepare me for the one He has for me. We both were guilty of adultery and destroying ourselves.

On the other hand, I know what it is to be an adulterous woman seeking affirmation outside of my marriage. I had married someone and later found out they were on the down low. The rejection and sexual disrespect during the marriage led me to suspect this may have been happening, and I even sought counsel

---

[13] Strong's Concordance; #5004 Niuph

from my pastor at that time. I was told that it would be better for me to be miserable for the rest of my life than to break the covenant of marriage. I tried to press through it, but ultimately, we separated, and during separation, I entered into a relationship with another man.

After a few months, I came to realize that this other man was a womanizer (that shouldn't have been a surprise to me). At one point, I remember praying and asking God to make this person love me, and I wanted God to hold him accountable for how he treated me. I wish you could hear me laughing as I type this because it is ridiculous that I would ever think that I could go to God about someone I was having an affair with. It doesn't matter if I was separated then; I was still married.

God will never give you someone else's husband, and He will never present you with a future spouse while you are married. I don't care how well you "vibe" they are not yours. That would be contrary to the character and righteousness of God.

HOMOSEXUALITY

My first encounter with the same sex was at five years old when a group of teenagers molested me. I and a family member were made to perform acts on each other. I've always had a competitive nature; I loved the attention and enjoyed the reaction I received, so I went above and beyond.

This is when I learned my body could be used for currency. It's when people-pleasing was instilled in me, and this is when the lines of love and acceptance were distorted. For years after, I was plagued with sex demons attacking me at night. They would hold me down, and I wouldn't be able to move or speak.

The enemy stole my innocence at a young age and replaced it with rejection. Rejection is so powerful in that it has an insatiable appetite for attention and competition – the more you "win" something, the more attention you receive, so you go to any length to get what you want. On top of that, rejection comes with some "friends;" they are the spirits of fear, shame, doubt, envy, jealousy, and more.

I was always afraid of not being enough, so I did whatever was necessary to be enough. Then, I would feel ashamed of my actions and afraid that someone would discover what I'd done. This led me to doubt myself and my intellect because why would I keep putting myself in these situations that always left me feeling empty? Doubt would then be overshadowed by envy because I would see someone with something that I wanted but felt I could never have – so I would find a placeholder for what I wanted, only to deal with the fear and jealousy that someone would take it from me.

Later in life, I explored because I was tired of being hurt by men, and I thought I could satisfy my desire for companionship while protecting my heart. This was a lie. I was left more broken.

MASTURBATION

There isn't a direct scripture in the Bible that says, "Thou shalt not pleasure thy self," and I used to believe it was okay to do it. I figured it wasn't fornication if there wasn't any penetration. Still, deep down, I didn't feel like I should be doing it because, eventually, it wasn't enough, and I would seek relief in other ways. So, I would try to stop. It wasn't easy because it was my "band-aid." I'd be proud of myself for going weeks at a time without doing it. Countless times, I gathered the courage to throw away my sex toys only to dig them out of the trash, sanitize them, and hide them in my closet.

Then, one day, about two months into my Man Fast, I thought about the fact that Holy Spirit dwells within me, and I asked God, "Where does Holy Spirit go when I do this?"

The thought of violating Holy Spirit or causing Him to leave me uncovered for even a second was frightening, so I stopped doing it. Cold Turkey. It was about two or three o'clock in the morning; I grabbed my sex toys and walked them to the dumpster at the end of my apartment building. Not the safest thing to do, but I was determined to push them as far out of my reach as possible.

Masturbation is a "gateway drug" to sexual immorality in that it ushers in the Spirit of Lust. The dictionary definition of lust is "*1) intense or unrestrained sexual craving, or 2) an overwhelming desire or craving*[14]." I've had women say to me, "I don't think about anything or anyone when I do it," that's a lie. Thoughts, sounds, feelings, and imagination stimulate us. That means that during the act, you are either fantasizing about someone you have been with, want to be with, or conjuring up a situation altogether. When that is not enough, many will turn to pornography while masturbating, and this invites the Lust of the Eyes (1 John 2:16).

PORNOGRAPHY

1 John 2:15,16 says, *[15] Do not love the world or the things in the world. If anyone loves the world, the love of the Father is not in him. [16] For all that is in the world—* **the lust of the flesh, the lust of the eyes, and the pride of life—** *is not of the Father but is of the world.* Pornography activates three things in this scripture that are clearly not of God and will separate us from Him:

A. **Lust of the Flesh**- is when natural sexual desires turn perverse; they lead to homosexuality, adultery, fornication, and other sexually related sins[15].

B. **Lust of the Eyes**- is the sinful desire to possess what we see or to have those things that have visual appeal[16].

---

[14] https://www.merriam-webster.com/dictionary/lust

[15] What Is Lust Of The Flesh? https://www.gotquestions.org/lust-of-the-flesh.html

[16] What Is Lust Of The Eyes? https://www.gotquestions.org/lust-of-the-eyes.html

C. **Pride of Life-** can be defined as anything that is "of the world," meaning anything that leads to arrogance, ostentation, pride in self, presumption, and boasting[17].

What is interesting is that some studies have found that pornography has been linked to low self-esteem, loneliness[18], severe or extremely severe levels of depression, anxiety, and stress[19]. This doesn't mean everyone who watches porn is dealing with these issues, but it's worth mentioning. When we look at the fact that watching pornography ushers in lust spirits that cause us to sin in our flesh, with our eyes, and feed our pride, it isn't surprising that some deal with this as an aftermath.

I was addicted to pornography. I was introduced to pornography at the age of 8. My parents have a powerful deliverance ministry, and they had been called to a woman's apartment to pray for her. For the young ones, this was the eighties, and you had to have cable or pay to access porn. It was late, around midnight, when her cable channel switched over to pornography, and I saw it for the first time. This was only a few years after my being molested, so you can

---

[17] What Is Pride Of Life? https://www.gotquestions.org/pride-of-life.html

[18] Loneliness, Pornography Use, Problematic Pornography Use, and Compulsive Sexual Behavior https://link.springer.com/article/10.1007/s40429-023-00516-0

[19] Compulsive Internet Pornography Use and Mental Health: A Cross-Sectional Study in a Sample of University Students in the United States https://pubmed.ncbi.nlm.nih.gov/33510691

see where the enemy was chasing me down; I only saw a few minutes before my father came out of prayer and turned the television off. The film was with two women, and I was hooked. Every chance I could, I would watch it. Back then, HBO would give free viewing days (I think they still do, but I barely watch television anymore, lol!). I would wait around for those times, stay up until my parents went to sleep, and watch it with the volume on mute.

As I grew into adulthood, porn was my escape from the loneliness of singlehood and, later, the loneliness of what felt like a loveless and often sexless marriage. While married, it went from being my "comfort" to my desire. I knew it was problematic when I realized that I was content with being ignored by my then-husband because I felt like I satisfied myself better with porn and masturbation anyway. When I was single and jumping from bed to bed, I would emulate what I saw, which fed my ego.

The bottom line is that pornography is a form of perversion. When God blesses you with your mate, the two of you will create a new, beautiful dynamic together. You should not be taking anyone into the bedroom with you – not past real-life partners nor the bad-acting partners from the pornography you've consumed.

Prayer To Break Soul Ties
(Pray audibly, even if it is a whisper)

Lord, I ask you to break all ungodly soul, spirit, body ties to (Name those you listed in the 'Pieces of Me' activity and any others you need to).

Lord, I ask that you remove the residue of all I have named. Wash and purify me with the blood of Jesus Christ. Every evil covenant that was established is destroyed and may the blood of Christ be payment for the breech.

I reject, renounce, denounce, and divorce myself from every known and unknown evil covenant and spiritual marriage made through masturbation, fornication, adultery, sodomy, homosexuality, lesbianism, lust, impurity, perversion, molestation, rape, all sexual abuse, and violations (list anything that may be missing).

In the name of Jesus, I reclaim my body, mind, soul, and spirit and give God full authority over all areas of my life.

Lord, I ask that you return to me every piece of my heart and body intended for my future husband.

I declare that every soul tie has been demolished in Jesus' Name!

There are gems in the word of God. Take time to study your word daily. Here is a list of scripture from within the chapter to get you started.

- 1 Corinthians 6:16 MSG
- Proverbs 6:32
- 1 John 2:15,16
- 2 Corinthians 10:4
- James 4:7
- 1 Thessalonians 4:1-18
- John 10:10

Lord, as I reflect on your word for my life, my thoughts are: _______________________________

____

____

____

____

____

____

____

____

____

The scripture(s) that resonated with me the most:

____
____
____
____
____
____
____
____
____
____

I will apply the scripture to my life by:

____
____
____
____
____
____
____
____
____

Chapter Ten

So, What Do I Do When I'm Horny?

I wasn't sure if I should give this chapter that title, but one day, a young woman searching for answers came to me and asked, "Dr. Hall, I'm trying to live right, but what do I do when I'm horny?"

It's a reality that we all face, and I decided not to sugarcoat it. What do *I* do? I apply the first sentence of 1 Corinthians 6:18, which says, *"Flee from sexual immorality..."* I run in the opposite direction.

The word "horny" simply means to want to have sex, to be sexually excited or sexually aroused. From a scientific perspective, sex feels so good because the brain releases a rush of Dopamine – a chemical that is part of the brain's reward system. We literally experience a rush of dopamine when we smell cookies baking, eat ice cream, or shop – anything that makes us feel rewarded[20]. We know that we can't eat a dozen of cookies without feeling sick, or spend our rent/mortgage on a pair of shoes without

---

[20] Dopamine: The Pathway to Pleasure, Watson, Stephanie; https://www.health.harvard.edu/mind-and-mood/dopamine-the-pathway-to-pleasure

consequences. If you've ever done either of those things, you learn quickly that it isn't a smart thing to do. It's the same with sex; you know how it impacts you when you engage in it out of proper context.

I know that I minimized sexual arousal by getting scientific with it, but the whole point is that you *can* control it. There is no easy fix for this, as this is a YOU problem. No one can conquer your flesh but you with God's help. 1 Corinthians 10:13 says, *No temptation has overtaken you except such as is common to man; but God is faithful, who will not allow you to be tempted beyond what you are able, but with the temptation will also make the way of escape, that you may be able to bear it.*

This verse means that God will provide a way of escape, but you have to take it. It will literally require you to exercise control over your flesh. You will need to be intentional about doing this. Listen, you can pray all day for God to help you, but the choice is yours at the end of the day.

I used to foolishly pray and ask God to stop me from having sex with someone while driving to their house after there had been a conversation and clear intention of our having sex. Was I serious? What did I expect God to do – take away the desire from me or the person I was going to see? I would literally ask God to provide a way of escape as I entered their home, took off my clothes, etc. Not taking personal responsibility for the fact that the way of escape was for me to *not* answer the phone in the first place (I already knew what was up). My escape route was to *not* get in my car and drive to their home. My escape was saying "no" and leaving at any moment before I had intercourse.

See, the enemy plays mind games with us. He makes us feel like we can't turn away from it because we've been tempted and possibly pursued the temptation. He makes us feel like we are already doomed because we've been tempted. Ever said, "Well, I'm already here now," before going forward with the act?

1 Corinthians 6:18, in its entirety, says, *"Flee from sexual immorality. All other sins a person commits are outside the body, but whoever sins sexually, sins against their own body."* And we just read the beginning of 1 Corinthians 10:13 which says, *"No temptation has overtaken you except such as is common to man..."*

Being horny is not a sin, being tempted is not a sin – but if it isn't put in check, it can lead to us engaging in sexual activity outside of the boundaries established by God – marriage. When we have sex outside of marriage, we defile our bodies and open the door to the enemy.

Sex has always been a destructive vice for me, so I knew that I had to get my flesh under control, and I took the following measures:

A. FASTING AND PRAYER AS A LIFESTYLE

Feeding your spirit and starving your flesh is a lifestyle of mine. When I first embarked on my Man Fast, I literally fasted for about five months straight. I did not eat until a specific time of day, and this helped me to discipline my flesh as I intentionally grew closer to God through prayer, reading my word, and abstaining from secular media. I was prepared to fast for the entire year if I had to, but one day, I woke up, and the Lord told me to stop.

Yes, I drew closer to God in that time, but I also learned to bring my flesh under subjection. Even now, if I feel myself getting weak, I will put myself on a fast. I talk to God, submit my fast to Him, and ask Him to honor it.

B. DON'T PLAY YOURSELF- YOU KNOW YOU CAN'T CONTROL YOURSELF!

Romans 13:14 says, *"Put on the Lord Jesus Christ, and make no provision for the flesh, to gratify its desires.* In other words, don't play yourself. If you know it's hard for you to control yourself, then you don't need to put yourself in situations where you can easily fall. For example, don't invite anyone to your home or go to someone's home when you know you lack self-control. Don't even test yourself; it isn't worth it.

C. LIMIT COMMUNICATION

During this time of fasting, it may be helpful for you to limit or eliminate communication altogether with potential mates. You're fasting, which can cause confusion and ultimately derail you from your fast. I realized early on that I couldn't have phone conversations with potential mates, especially those I was already familiar with, because the conversation always went in the wrong direction. So, I didn't have phone conversations or go on dates at all.

What is a potential mate? For me, it's ANYONE outside of my family, true friends, and business colleagues. Listen, people that you wouldn't normally find attractive become eye candy with the right conversation and attention.

D. PROTECT YOUR EYE AND EAR GATES

Filter what you are watching and the music you are listening to. I will literally fast-forward through romance scenes in a movie, television show, or audiobook. I don't actively listen to secular music anymore, but when I first started the fast, I would occasionally listen to an artist I liked. I stopped that immediately because, to be honest, the songs I liked were sexual in nature. They reminded me of past encounters, made me daydream about future sexcapades, and evoked sexual feelings.

E. DON'T PARTICIPATE IN AROUSING ACTIVITIES

In addition to steering clear of obvious activities like masturbation, I also ran from situations that were sexually charged. For example, a few years ago, one of my friends hosted a pole dancing class for her birthday. Initially, I signed up to go but changed my mind a month later after making the decision to abstain from sex. I'm a dancer and have always enjoyed dancing for a man – so to attend a pole dancing class would have awakened the very feelings I was fighting.

Everyone is different, and only you know the activities that arouse you. Whatever they are, stay away from them. Point – Blank – Period!

F. PRAY AND REFOCUS

It may sound really churchy, but yes, I pray. For me, my days are so busy that nighttime is when I have moments. So, when my flesh is hot, and I'm having difficulty, I will ask God to help me go to sleep and force myself to think of other things, and usually, it doesn't take me long to fall asleep.

The chapter asks the question, "So, what do I do when I'm horny?" What do I do? I apply the first sentence of 1 Corinthians 6:18, which says, *"Flee from sexual immorality...."* **I run in the opposite direction of my sexual triggers, no matter how "harmless" they may seem.**

Be honest with yourself about what your sexual triggers are so that you can establish boundaries for yourself. You can't expect someone else to do it; you have to control yourself.

The Sex Escape Plan

During a Man Fast, you should abstain from dating altogether, but that doesn't mean feelings won't arise, or people won't pursue you. In fact, you may find that you are being pursued more now that you're fasting than when you were available. It's good to identify your sexual triggers and flush out how you will control them and ultimately escape from sexual immorality.

SEXUAL TRIGGERS

When I think about sexual triggers, I think of foreplay or outercourse. Foreplay is any sexual activity that takes place before intercourse - even though sexual intercourse doesn't have to occur. I divide foreplay into two different trigger categories – Obvious and Sneaky.

The **obvious triggers** are those involving physical touch and interaction, like kissing and touching, grinding, etc. I don't need to give any more detail, do I? You can fill the rest in. The sneaky triggers are those that seem harmless, like talking, cuddling, holding hands, etc. People are aroused differently, so it's important to know yourself so that you don't fall into any traps during your fast and after.

1. What are your **OBVIOUS** sexual triggers?

____

____

____

____

2. What are your **SNEAKY** triggers?

____

____

____

____

BOUNDARIES:

Establish boundaries for yourself *NOW*. Writing them down will give you a point of reference when you are confronted by a situation. For example, during my time of fasting, I connected to someone who was hilarious and pretty much everything I'd been looking for in a mate. I hadn't spoken to a man on the phone in eight months, and we began to chat as friends. I soon realized my attraction for him and how I said we were friends but kept slipping into "dating" actions and my natural flirtatious ways. So, I reviewed the plan I'd created while writing this book and immediately shut the conversations down. He was completely amazing, but I'd promised to give God a year with no distractions.

3. What will you do to *flee* from your triggers?

____

____

____

4. Are you flirty? If yes, what boundaries do you need to establish for your actions?

____

____

____

5. What will you say to someone who broaches the idea of having sex?

____

____

____

6. How will you handle a friendship that pushes the limits beyond friendship?

____

____

____

7. How will you handle a phone conversation or text that becomes too intimate? What will you say?

____

____

____

8. If you find yourself breaching your established boundaries, how will you quickly reset?

____

____

____

Prayer For Strength Of Sexual Boundaries
(Pray audibly, even if it is a whisper)

Lord, thank you for my redeemer, shield, protector during my Man Fast. Today, I lay my sexual proclivities, desires, and weaknesses at your feet. I declare that they will no longer control my actions or rule my thoughts (Romans 13:14)

Lord, as our relationship grows, I give you full authority and ask that you guide my footsteps that I do not step into evil territory. Should I find myself in a space of temptation, please give me the strength to remove myself.

Lord, I ask that you give me the courage to stick to my spiritual convictions so that I may not be overtaken by temptation (1 Corinthians 10:13).

Lord, I ask that you help me to quickly take every thought and potential action captive so that I may resist the Devil, his sneaky ways, and flee from all sexual immorality (1 Corinthians 6:18, 2 Corinthians 10:5).

____

____

____

____

____

____

There are gems in the word of God. Take time to study your word daily. Here is a list of scripture from within the chapter to get you started.

- 1 Corinthians 6:18-20
- 1 Corinthians 10:13
- Romans 13:14
- 2 Corinthians 10:4,5
- Ephesians 6:10-20
- Joshua 6:1–27
- 1 Peter 5:5,6

Lord, as I reflect on your word for my life, my thoughts are: _______________________________

____

____

____

____

____

____

____

____

____

The scripture(s) that resonated with me the most:

____
____
____
____
____
____
____
____
____

I will apply the scripture to my life by:

____
____
____
____
____
____
____
____
____

PART IV
Becoming The Good Thing

This section requires you to go deep and to be selfish about your healing. This section will get you ready for the relationship God has for you, but it is solely about you, the woman, and becoming who you were born to be. By the time you finish this section, my prayer is that you will be so confident in your identity as THE Good Thing that you trust God with your mate. Your future mate will have no choice but to go through God to get to you.

Chapter Eleven
Five Promises OF Righteous Living

Let's just be real; it can seem difficult to turn away from things that you naturally want. Righteous living doesn't always feel good and doesn't always appear to be easy – *in the beginning.* If you make righteousness a lifestyle and not a passing moment, you will find that your Spirit Man will take over.

In other words, when you allow Holy Spirit to lead your life, His voice will begin to speak louder than your flesh (Romans 8:14). It isn't that God doesn't speak to us; most of the time, we don't listen. Sometimes, we are so distracted by what we want or the drama of getting what we want and not what we need that we don't hear him.

Don't get it twisted; though Holy Spirit will lead us, it still requires intention, but you will desire to be *in right standing* with God. You'll find that not only does it *not* feel good to do your own thing, but it doesn't feel *safe* to let your flesh control your movements. Who wants to exist in the aftermath of sexual sin? Who wants to deal with the conviction that comes from lying, keeping secrets, and living in darkness?

As hard as it may *feel*, there are benefits or promises that come with righteous living. Notice I used the words "as hard as it may <u>feel</u>" and not "as hard as it may *be*." The reality is that our feelings/emotions are temporal. They are fleeting. Our flesh loves to reside within our emotions, and feelings do not always lead us to what is good for us and what is right.

Satan appeals to our flesh and casts doubt to make us believe that there is no benefit to living holy. Satan will magnify a mistake we've made and amplify the shame so that we feel unworthy and without redemption so that we don't seek after God. It's a lie! God loves you. God has an assignment for you. And it doesn't matter what you've done; you can be used to bring Him Glory. Honeyyyyyy, I am a witness!

I want to share with you some of the promises of righteous living by diving into the Word.

PROMISE #1
God Will Reward You For Your Obedience

... Do not be afraid, Abram, I am your shield; <u>Your reward [for obedience] shall be very great.</u>
Genesis 15:1 AMP

To put this passage in context, Abraham (at this point, he was still Abram.) had just finished a fierce battle to save his nephew, Lot (Genesis 14). He was fearful as we read into Genesis 15. In the first verse, God reassures Abraham that he will protect him and that he will be **rewarded** for his obedience.

Some may not understand the significance of this because we often use the words award and reward synonymously, but they are different. An *award* is given to someone to recognize their achievement. For example, an athlete may receive a trophy for scoring the most points in a season. A teacher may receive an award as a teacher of the year. A *reward* is given to someone due to their actions – not their achievement.

God established a covenant relationship with Abraham that he would give him security, protection, and blessings, and more descendants than he could count[21]. Singleness and righteousness can be scary – especially if you are choosing to approach relationships differently than you ever have. As someone who used her body to determine if someone cared for me or not, in the beginning, it was unnerving to believe that by not giving myself to someone, I would increase my value. But just as God established a covenant relationship with Abraham, He did the same for me, and I trust Him with my heart.

It is a promise that God *will reward you* for your obedience.

---

[21]How is God an exceedingly great reward (Genesis 15:1)? https://www.gotquestions.org/exceedingly-great-reward.html

PROMISE #2
The Righteous Will Thrive
The righteous shall flourish like a palm tree.
–Psalm 92:12 (NKJV).

When you are in right standing with God, you will flourish, you will thrive. From a natural perspective, the Palm Tree is significant in that it is a beautiful tree that produces fruit and grows toward Heaven- no matter how much weight it may carry, it reaches upward[22]. Spiritually, we may go through storms and experience the weight of life – but we will always come out on top. We will always thrive. We don't look like what we've been through, we will produce and, yes, thrive in adversity.

PROMISE #3
God Listens To the Prayers of The Righteous

The eyes of the Lord are over the righteous, and his ears are open unto their prayers. –1 Peter 3:12 (KJV)

The righteous cry and the Lord hears, and delivers them out of all their troubles." –Psalm 34:17 (NKJV)

---

[22] W. Clarkson; The Significance of Palm Trees; https://biblehub.com/sermons/auth/clarkson/the_significance_of_the_p alm_trees.htm

The righteous can be confident that God will hear their prayers and assured that He is watching over them.

PROMISE #4
The Righteous Will Be Delivered
*The **seed** of the righteous shall be delivered.*
–Proverbs 11:21 (KJV)

This means that everything that comes from you will be delivered. You can live with confidence that God is going to deliver you and your children; the seed you sow will bloom, and you will not be held captive by the Enemy.

PROMISE #5
You Will Be Blessed With Favor
You, O Lord, will bless the righteous; with favor, You will surround him as with a shield.
–Psalm 5:12 (NKJV).

Favor is released to the righteous. This means that God will open doors for you that man says you are not worthy or qualified to walk through, but because you have *FAVOR* you will walk in supernatural approval. The favor that will rest on your life will act as a shield against the weapons of the enemy.

There are a number of scriptures that point to the benefit of righteous living, but these are just a few for you to consider. Being in right standing with God allows us to freely walk in Proverbs 3:5-6. The Amplified Bible says, *Trust in and rely confidently on the LORD with all your heart. And do not rely on your own insight or understanding. In all your ways, know and acknowledge and recognize Him, And He will make your paths straight and smooth [removing obstacles that block your way].*

In life, we will experience obstacles. **When we are in right standing with God, we can have the confidence that obstacles designed to block our path will be removed.**

Reflection

After studying some of the promises of righteous living, what thoughts do you have?

____

____

____

____

____

____

____

____

____

____

____

____

____

____

____

____

____

____

Prayer For Righteous Living
(Pray audibly, even if it is a whisper)

Lord, I thank you for your presence in my life during this fast. Thank you for being a keeper, for destroying yokes in my life, for breaking curses off of my life, and for redeeming me.

As I continue in this fast, Lord, I that as I seek you and press into your presence, make me more like you. May I receive life, prosperity, and honor according to Proverbs 21:21.

Lord, my heart and desires have shifted since I've turned down my plate and brought my flesh under subjection. Please fortifiy my faith that I never be shaken by materialistc things, nor tempted by my flesh (Psalm 112:6; Matthew 6:33).

Lord, I fix my thoughts on what is true, honorable, right, pure, lovely, and admirable. I will think about things that are excellent and worthy of praise (Philippians 4:8).

Lord, create in me a clean heart. Let righteousness motivate all of my actions (Psalm 51:10; Matthew 6:33). May my spoken words and unspoken thoughts be acceptable in your sight (Psalm 19:14).

____

____

____

____

There are gems in the word of God. Take time to study your word daily. Here is a list of scripture from within the chapter to get you started.

- Romans 8:14
- *Genesis 15:1 AMP*
- *Psalm 92:12*
- *1 Peter 3:12*
- *Psalm 34:17*
- *Proverbs 11:21 (KJV)*
- *Psalm 5:12 (NKJV)*

Lord, as I reflect on your word for my life, my thoughts are: ______________________________

____

____

____

____

____

____

____

____

The scripture(s) that resonated with me the most:

____

____

____

____

____

____

____

____

____

____

I will apply the scripture to my life by:

____

____

____

____

____

____

____

____

____

Chapter Twelve
You Are Good Merchandise!

Six months before I started writing this book, I was preparing to preach at a women's conference in Canada when the Lord had a sweet, fatherly conversation with me. He said:

- ♥ My daughters have forgotten that they are heirs to the throne.
- ♥ They have allowed others to diminish their value.
- ♥ They walk with their heads low.
- ♥ They have forgotten that they don't have to accept just anything.
- ♥ They look good in public, confident in public, but behind closed doors, they battle low self-esteem, depression, suicidal thoughts, and shame, they have forgotten who they are, or perhaps they never knew. Instead of rest, they seek relief from a bottle.

So, I began seeking out what the *issue* was. I asked, "Papa, is it a heart issue?"

He responded, "It's a *worth* issue. They don't understand their worth."

We love to quote Proverbs 18:22, *"He who finds a wife finds a good thing, and obtains favor from the Lord" (NKJV),* but there is a difference between quoting scripture and knowing with the very fabric of your being that you are indeed a good thing. Becoming the good thing means to come in agreement with your identity in Christ, to believe that you are indeed who God says you are.

The Enemy has been on a mission to steal our identity. He pulls us away from God when we don't know *who we are* when we fall away from *who we were* in God, and when *we don't walk in our calling.*

THE PLACE CALLED *"THERE!"*

I want to take a moment to talk to you about a place called *there*. I'm not necessarily referring to a physical place, though it could be, but I'm talking about a place locked within. A hidden place we go as a result of hurt, disappointment, bad decisions, etc. We don't usually recognize that we are traveling to this place until we have arrived and we don't know how we got there.

The Lord showed me a place called *THERE*. I found myself deep in a dark hole, a place with tight walls, a sunken place. Where I could see the light above me, but there was no way for me to get out. In this place called *THERE* it felt like a prison. People were all around, and yet I felt isolated. It was solitary confinement within oneself – a place where I, as a woman, operated robotically through life. I looked fine to everyone around me, but I felt invisible.

Ever felt like this? You're someone's mother, wife, employee, boss, and minister - and yet you still feel invisible. You exist simply to meet everyone else's needs – but your own needs don't matter. And in this place, it doesn't matter how beautifully you dress, keep your hair done, or face beat, and yet, when you look in the mirror, you don't recognize the woman staring back at you, and you wonder how you got *THERE*.

The Enemy has been working so hard to make you feel invisible because he knows that if you locate your identity, you'll discover your worth. **Proverbs 31:10 asks, "Who can find a virtuous wife? For Her worth is far above rubies."**

**And Proverbs 31:18 responds,
"She perceiveth that her merchandise is good: Her candle goeth not out by night."**

What you say to yourself matters. How you see yourself matters. Most interpret this scripture to mean that the virtuous woman creates merchandise and sells it – and that is true, but for a moment, I'd like you to consider that *you* are the merchandise, and how you perceive yourself, what you think about yourself...matters.

Before the earth was even created, God established your worth. You've been stuck in a place called THERE because:

- **You've been feeling like you aren't good enough, but Genesis 1:31** lets us know that it wasn't until woman was created that God stood back, looked at what He had created, and said it was "VERY GOOD."
- **You hate your looks, and your shape, but Ephesians 2:10** declares that you are God's masterpiece. His favorite piece of art.

You've shackled to a place called *THERE* because

- **You've been told that you are too difficult by small-minded people when Psalm 139:14** says that you are marvelously complex.

And the moment you begin to feel overtaken in the place called THERE, God sent me here to tell you that one of the most valuable gemstones was created in a place called THERE and compared your value to it.

- **Proverbs 31:10 asks Who can find a virtuous wife; her worth is far above rubies.**

THE RUBY AND YOU...A Valuable Comparison!

I want to take a moment and give you a geology lesson, so to speak, and talk to you about the Ruby. A ruby is more rare than a diamond because of how they are created. Special conditions are needed; it is created deep in the earth's crust with two ingredients: corundum and aluminum oxide (in a place called "there").

Rubys are formed under extreme heat and pressure. (Have you ever felt like you were under intense heat or pressure in life?). It takes 20 to 30 million years to develop a ruby. That means that when the earth was created, God established the value of your worth. As a matter of fact, if we were to travel to Genesis 1:3, that's when the Lord separated the dry land from the waters. Your value was extracted on the third day; before Adam was even created, your value was increasing.

Sis, do you realize this means that God compared your worth to something that takes 20-30 million years, extreme heat, and pressure to create? Listen, it took a lot for you to be here. I know that some days you've had to fight just to get out of bed, take your hair off the dresser, put on your clothes, and show up for the day. God saw the nights you cried and watched how you managed to carry the pressure. The pressure wasn't meant to overtake you; it increased you're worth!

Here's what's interesting about ruby creation. Remember, it's found in the earth's crust, in the same place sand and iron are found. Now understand that while a ruby is very rare, sand and iron are very plentiful and extremely common, and they are found in the same place where rubies are created. Catch this: if sand or iron comes anywhere near the minerals needed to form a ruby, it won't be created – so the ruby that is created somewhere down *there* has to somehow be separated from the ordinary/common thing.

Let me give it to you this way. The ruby... The valuable thing... is created *THERE*, deep in a dirty place, a commonplace, surrounded by ordinary things, and yet it is isolated. Instead of simply staying buried, the ingredients that seem worthless on their own begin to gather themselves together. They pull together to create what is known as one of the most rare gems found on earth.

Every woman has a *THERE*. You know where your *THERE* is, and I've been sent here to tell you that your brokenness is mending together, fusing together, and increasing in value.

It's a matter of perspective. The enemy designed you to die in *THERE,* but God was molding and shaping you in the dark moments. You are the good merchandise, but you have to perceive it/know it for yourself. It doesn't matter who doesn't see your value or who leaves you *THERE* because they thought you didn't deserve any better.

Where is your place of *THERE*? Mine was isolation, loneliness, depression, rage, shame, doubt, jealousy, low self-esteem, and self-hate. My THERE was a place full of abuse, sexual abuse, and rejection...but then I perceived it differently...I thought to myself...I gathered myself; I got myself together in *THERE*. I allowed God to tell me who I was. He showed me my value. I began to look at myself in the mirror and say, "Girl, you're a dime piece."

I learned how to set boundaries and that I'm allowed to have expectations in my place called *THERE*. I learned to love my own company, and I found healing. There doesn't have to be a dead place; it can be your place of development, a place where God will feed your spirit if you allow Him to. But you can't stay *THERE*. You're good merchandise. You're too valuable.

Remember that you are a ruby, but no one will ever experience the fullness of the ruby if it stays buried.

Prayer For Becoming The Good Thing

(Pray audibly, even if it is a whisper)

Father, thank you for the gift of calling you Abba. It is an honor to be your daughter and a gift to be loved by You. I ask that you forgive me for the times I looked at myself in the mirror and didn't like my reflection. Everything you created is wonderfully made and that includes me (Psalm 139:14).

Today, I take my rightful place as heir to the throne (Romans 8:17). No longer will I allow others to diminish my value, including myself.

Lord, while in this wait, please guide me. I lay all hurt, distrust, insecurities, at your feet. I turn all career, financial, credit, children, and household affairs over to you that when I am joined to my husband, I will be an asset and not a burden (Proverbs 31)

I declare Proverbs 18:22 is fully activated in my life. I am a good thing and favor follows me. I am a good thing. I am good merchandise, and the man you are preparing for me will love me as such (Proverbs 31:18).

____

____

____

____

____

There are gems in the word of God. Take time to study your word daily. Here is a list of scripture from within the chapter to get you started.

- Proverbs 18:22
- Proverbs 31
- Romans 8:17
- Psalm 139:14

Lord, as I reflect on your word for my life, my thoughts are: _______________________________

____

____

____

____

____

____

____

____

____

The scripture(s) that resonated with me the most:

____

____

I will apply the scripture to my life by:

Chapter Thirteen
THE 10 I AM, I AM Nots

Matters of the heart have always been an issue for me. It has been a source of distraction and stagnation. Part of the reason is because I always played a position in someone's life that was never given to me. I was quick to slip into the role of wifey as soon as I thought someone was husband material. I would do it to prove that I could fill the role, but I was always left depleted.

As I allowed God to heal the fragmented pieces of my self-esteem that gave easy access to my heart, I learned to guard my heart with some identity truth.

1. **I AM trusting God with my heart. Anyone who wants to be with me must go through God first.** Queen, you've labored to be here. You've denied yourself, faced yourself in the mirror, and allowed God to process you. Don't you dare give yourself to someone who hasn't done the same.

2. **I *AM* A Wife; I AM *NOT* Your Wife Until You Put A Ring On It**. Yes, you ARE a wife. Knowing that is powerful because it helps you establish how you

want to be treated. You will date with purpose when you know that you *are* a wife; however, the person you date has not earned the right to experience wifey benefits from you, so be careful not to give that away freely.

3. **I *AM* Alone; I Am *NOT* Desperate.** Right now, you are alone by choice. Don't forget that you have chosen to be on this fast. You could be dating anyone whether they are right for you or not, but you have chosen yourself in this season. That is significant in how you view the moments when you may feel lonely.

    In the beginning, I felt lonely quite a bit, but as my relationship with God grew, I appreciated my value, and now I enjoy my own company. I can be alone and not feel the painful sting of loneliness – but I do have my moments, and that's okay. When you have that moment, remind yourself that you have chosen to put yourself first and that you are not desperate for companionship that doesn't serve you.

4. **I *AM* a Help Meet, I AM *NOT* A Garbage Can:** Help Meets were created to "fill in the blanks" of their spouse, whether that is financial, spiritual, emotional, etc. Marriage requires a level of selflessness that only makes sense for two people who have pledged their lives to each other.

    The mistake many of us make is giving away wifely benefits to someone we are dating or not dating as a way to prove we are worthy of a ring and permanent placement.

Be careful not to become someone's garbage can. You become a garbage can when someone takes advantage of your wifely benefits without the commitment of marriage.

What do we do with garbage cans? We toss our waste in them and walk away. No one hangs out around a garbage can; its purpose is to collect unwanted things from people who need to lighten their load. We allow ourselves to be treated like waste baskets when we allow people to mentally, emotionally, and financially dump their issues on us; sexually, they dump their bodies into us (I don't need to be any more specific), and they feel better once they have finished and we are left to clean up the mess.

5. **I *AM* the FIRST CHOICE; I Am *NOT* A Placeholder or an Option**. A **placeholder** is a person or thing that occupies the position or place of another person or thing[23]. An **option** is when there are multiple people or things being considered.

When you date with a purpose, you've decided on an ending goal. In most cases, it's marriage. You are more valuable than needing to audition to be relationship-worthy or being treated as a placeholder, simply occupying space until the person they want comes along.

---

[23] https://www.merriam-webster.com/dictionary/placeholder

Establishing personal boundaries is important because it helps you determine what is right for you. On a personal level, I don't entertain someone who is dating multiple people; I don't like how it makes me feel, and I'm just not interested in that. I have never cared to date aimlessly for a free meal because I can buy my own meals and take myself on trips. I refuse to compete for someone's affection.

6. **I *AM* MORE THAN ENOUGH; I AM *NOT* lacking in anything.** You've been made to feel that you aren't good enough to be loved, and so you've been comparing yourself to people around you- when, in reality, God didn't feel as though creation was complete until you – the woman was created, and only after that did He look at all that He had made and said, "It was VERY good" -Genesis 1:31.

7. **I AM The Someone He Is Praying For Right Now; I Am *NOT* going to be single forever.** One lie the enemy tells women in waiting is, "You're going to be single forever." This lie compels many of us to accept the first person who gives us attention and/or wallow in self-pity and be a slave to loneliness.

   In knowing that you are worthy of love and that you are THE good thing, you will have to trust that God is completing the work in your partner just as He is in you. If you have the desire to be married, know that God gave that desire to you, and rest in the fact that there is a man who is praying for you to enter his life.

8. **I AM Worth The Wait; I am *NOT* required to give my mind, body, or heart until I am ready and believe they have proven themselves worthy.**
It may seem hard to believe, but the right man is to fight for you. He will not want you to get away, and he will do what is necessary to be worthy of you in his life. You are worth the wait. You are worth the "work" it takes to get close to you. Everyone does not deserve to be intimate (close) with you. You need to be able to trust a person with your secrets and the brilliance of your mind. Remember that your heart matters and your body should be the last on the list. By now, we've learned that the body "seals" the contract. There is a covenant created when two people bind themselves together.

9. **I AM a woman with standards, expectations, and boundaries. I am *NOT* bending to suit the needs of others.** You've been told that your standards are too high and no one could ever meet them. Listen, you were created to reproduce and nurture; God made sure that everything you would need would be laid out before you. It's in your DNA to have expectations. It doesn't matter what you may or may not have accepted in the past, your standards, expectations, and boundaries are what matter now.

10. I AM favor. The Bible says, "He That Findeth A Wife Findeth A Good Thing, and Obtains FAVOR from the Lord." I am *NOT* going to squander the favor on my life ever again. I know, I know, this was a long "I Am" commandment, but hey, it needed to be said! Remember that favor is attached to you – everyone attached to you wins, and don't just give that away to a person who has not proven themselves.

This next time you allow someone in your life, let God lead.

Reflection

Add your own "I Am, I Am Not" Statements.

Prayer To Release Joy & Christ Declarations
(Pray audibly, even if it is a whisper)

Lord, thank you for being the source of my joy and strength (Nehemiah 8:10). What may have begun as a hard thing (the Man Fast), is coming to a close with Joy.

Lord, I choose to abide in your love by keeping your commandments and living righteously. I come into full agreement with your love that says I am fearfully and wonderfully made (Psalm 139:14), I am the apple of your eye (Psalm 17:8, Zecheriah 2:8). And because of this:

- I Am called, restored, strong, firm, and steadfast in Christ (1 Peter 5:10)
- I Am chosen and appointed by you to bear fruit (John 15:16)
- I Am your favorite piece of art (Ephesians 2:10)
- I Am Blessed, favored, and filled with joy (Ephesians 1:3; Job 10:12; John 17:3)
- I Am confident that You will finish a good work in me (Philippians 1:6).

____

____

____

____

____

____

____

There are gems in the word of God. Take time to study your word daily. Here is a list of scripture from within the chapter to get you started.

- Nehemiah 8:10
- Psalm 17:8
- Ephesians 1:3
- Job 10:12
- John 17:3
- Philippians 1:6
- John 15:16

Lord, as I reflect on your word for my life, my thoughts are: _______________________________

____

____

____

____

____

____

____

____

The scripture(s) that resonated with me the most:

I will apply the scripture to my life by:

Chapter Fourteen
Saved, Single, & Not Settling

I'm writing this last chapter on December 30, 2023, as I have promised the Lord to finish this book before the year is complete. Today, my father asked me about the lessons I've learned while on this fast and if I knew when the change took place in my life. I answered Him and started from the end of my fast, took him to my mindset at the beginning, and finished with my feelings of today.

On October 24, 2023, I completed my Man Fast. I didn't even realize it until that evening when Holy Spirit reminded me. I was standing in my kitchen about to cook, and I had a random thought about what it would be like to cook for my husband one day when the date was brought to my attention. I took a moment to thank God for keeping through the fast. I asked Him to honor my sacrifice, and then I told Him, "Papa, until *YOU* tell me I am released to date, I'm rocking with you!"

It's funny because when God first told me to go on the fast, I immediately said "yes," only to have a breakdown hours later, thinking that another year of singleness was just too much to ask me, only to release my anxiety and dive into the fast head first. There were a few moments when I wanted God to speed up the time, only to now be fully surrendered to His will for my life. Now, I completely trust God with my heart, and I don't mind waiting. He knows what's best for me.

The Lord has also shown me how much of a protector and revealer He is. Anyone who showed an interest, and I mean *anyone*, the Lord was the "truth serum." I've said a few times during this book that men may pursue you. Listen, there is a glory that will surround you when you are in the presence of the Lord. People will be drawn to you and not even understand why. Your beauty will be amplified because of the glory that walks with you. Because of this, some can't help but show an interest.

This served as a boot camp of sorts for me. This year, my ministry engagements took me all over the world, and I ministered in the United States as well as four different countries. I met a lot of people and, of course, came across "Godly" men who expressed an interest. In polite conversation, the Lord would quickly reveal the cracks in their façade from being married, baby mama drama, and sex addictions to those who have a form of godliness but no real commitment to doing the will of the Father. Sometimes, the Holy Spirit would impress upon me what the person was hiding, and I would ask (the expression on their faces, lol!); other times, all I had to do was sit back and listen to them spill their secrets. This didn't take long, usually a few minutes.

My boundaries have expanded. God taught me that anyone who is interested in me will have to go through Him first. They will have to pass the Papa test! Perfection isn't necessary, but I fought for my deliverance, and I don't believe that God had me go through this process to be with someone who has not given Him a surrendered "yes." That's what the Man Fast requires: a *surrendered* yes. That "yes" takes strength and courage. It means that you intentionally deny your desires, cravings, and fleshly needs to do the will of the Father.

Sis, don't forfeit your promise to someone who is too weak to give God a true "yes." The potential of a person is not enough. The man God is preparing for you will be ready. You will not have to "mother" him into position. He will follow God, so he will be able to lead you. The two of you will fulfill purpose together, build kingdom together, without jealousy or competion. Demons will tremble at the power of your union because, *one can chase a thousand, two can put ten thousand to flight* (Deuteronomy 32:30).

I am proud that I did not give up on myself or the fast. My healing was worth the wait. During this year, I have been delivered from my addiction to pornography and masturbation. Initially, I thought they were the only way for me to cope with my flesh, but I have learned how to rule my flesh and not allow it to control me. I will always keep my flesh in check. The flesh doesn't want us to do good, and it doesn't care about the fact that I'm a preacher; it will lead me astray.

I don't purposely tempt my flesh and will flee a conversation or location quickly.

After all of that, my final answer to the change God has orchestrated in my life is that I, who used to prostitute herself for attention, am fulfilled by the presence of God. I am content to wait for the Lord to bring me together with my mate. I am Saved, Single, & Not Settling for less than God's best for me.

Final Reflection

What lessons have you learned since the beginning of your fast?

____

____

____

____

____

____

____

____

____

____

____

____

____

____

____

____

____

____

____

____

When or how have you recognized the change in your life?

Finish the statement: I am proud that...

____

____

____

____

____

____

____

____

____

____

____

Finish the statement: I will continue to keep the following in check...

____

____

____

____

____

____

____

____

____

____

Prayer Of Completion
(Pray audibly, even if it is a whisper)

Lord, I thank you that with your help I have successfully completed my Man Fast. During this time I have learned: ________________________

____

____

____

Our relationship has grown so much and not only do I see you as God, but I have come to know you as my Heavenly father, _______________________

____

____

Lord, I ask that you keep while I am waiting on the next in my life. Please help to keep the following in check: _

____

____

____

____

The next phase of my life is completely in your hands. Please complete the work in my future spouse and allow me to be found by Him at the appointed time.

____

____

____

There are gems in the word of God. Take time to study your word daily. Here is a list of scripture from within the chapter to get you started.

- Deuteronomy 32:30
- Psalm 30:2
- Isaiah 41:10
- Jeremiah 17:14
- Ephesians 1:4-6
- Hebrews 12:1
- Hebrews 11

Lord, as I reflect on your word for my life, my thoughts are: _______________________

____

____

____

____

____

____

____

____

The scripture(s) that resonated with me the most:

____
____
____
____
____
____
____
____
____
____
____

I will apply the scripture to my life by:

____
____
____
____
____
____
____
____
____
____
____

D r. Tamika Hall has been called a Thought Leader and Spiritual General of our time. She empowers women worldwide in the areas of leadership, business, and personal development. A Certified Christian Counselor, she is affectionately known as "The Purpose Bully" and mentors women through her ministry, She Wins By Faith.

A digital media mogul, she is the CEO of Tamika INK Media Group, home to TamikaINK Publishing & PR, She Wins Media.

Former CEO of iWorship96 FM Radio, Tamika's voice can be heard through her weekly programs:

Speak Over Yourself Podcast, The Man Fast Podcast, and Sleeptime and Bible.

The internationally bestselling author of more than 20 books, twelve of which have held the number one spot on Amazon's Bestseller's List, including the internationally bestselling "She Wins By Faith Anthology Series," which has featured more than 100 women from around the world.

Former model and pageant queen, many days, you will find Tamika styling and directing photoshoots for ministers, entrepreneurs, and artists.

In September 2020, Tamika launched Smell Pretty Co., A company that produces plant-based deodorant capsules and gummies that fight bad breath, stinky armpits, vagina odor, and smelly feet. The capsules have been shipped all over the United States, Japan, Malaysia, South Africa, Jamaica, and Denmark.

Adding filmmaker to her growing list of accomplishments, Tamika made history as the first African-American woman to release a full-length film, She Wins Beyond the Bruises, on August 28, 2021.

Stay Connected!

www.tamikahall.com

Instagram, Facebook, Tik Tok:
@iamtamikahall1

Youtube:
www.youtube.com/@TamikaHall